UNVEILINGS
A Desert Jou

Patricia A

CONTENTS

DEDICATION

SECTION ONE
Beginning the Journey

INTRODUCTION
GETTING TO RIYADH
MIDDLE EAST PREVIEW

SECTION TWO
Stories Along the Way

CHAPTER 1 -- MY LIFE IN RIYADH -- Riyadh, Saudi Arabia -- 1976
CHAPTER 2 -- MY DESERT HOME -- Riyadh, Saudi Arabia -- 1976
CHAPTER 3 -- MY DESERT CHURCH -- Riyadh, Saudi Arabia -- 1976
CHAPTER 4 -- TEMPORARY ESCAPE -- Italy and Germany -- 1976
CHAPTER 5 -- MY DESERT ROUTINE -- Riyadh, Saudi Arabia -- 1977
CHAPTER 6-- EXPANDING HORIZONS -- Riyadh, Saudi Arabia -- 1977
CHAPTER 7 -- CHANGING TIMES -- Riyadh, Saudi Arabia -- 1977
CHAPTER 8 -- GETTING TO EGYPT --Cairo and Alexandria, Egypt -- 1978
CHAPTER 9 -- OVERCOMING HURDLES -- Riyadh, Saudi Arabia -- 1978
CHAPTER 10 -- SOUTHERN ROOTS -- Riyadh, Saudi Arabia -- 1978
CHAPTER 11 -- DARK CLOUDS GATHERING -- Riyadh, Saudi Arabia -- 1979
CHAPTER 12 -- ISRAEL -- Tel Aviv, Israel -- 1981-82
CHAPTER 13 -- TRANSITIONS

SECTION THREE
Unveiled

THE OTHER SIDE OF THE DESERT
POLITICAL OVERVIEW
US-SAUDI ARABIA ALLIANCE

ALL RIGHTS TO THIS BOOK BELONG T0:
PATRICIA ADORA CLARK TAYLOR

COPYRIGHT OFFICE   US LIBRARY OF CONGRESS   WASHINGTON, DC

FEBRUARY 4, 2004
TXu-160-519

SECTION ONE
Beginning the Journey

UNVEILINGS
A Desert Journey
by
Patricia Adora Clark Taylor

INTRODUCTION
About the Journey

As an artist, I view the Middle East through a prism and envision layers of time painted in bright daylight colors, together with deepest dark-of-night colors. It is the only way I can look at the Middle East. In my mind, the Middle East is a work of art containing the sharp edges of logic and reason, together with water color emotion that smears across the sharpest lines, eluding the viewer.

What is the viewer to make of this place, this political landscape painted upon ancient multi-colored-rocks, jutting up from streams that cut through the dry desert like slender fingers? I want to know the artist who painted this incredible painting. Perhaps many artists left their footprints, their special touch upon the canvas. It is a canvas painted in contrasts. There are dark places upon the canvas soaked in blood; but viewed from a different angle, one can see the brilliant sound of song, laugher, and jingling gold bracelets piercing the darkness. There is a mosque with a gold dome painted upon a holy rock; there is a pyramid jutting up from the desert, one of the original Seven Wonders of the World. Painted upon the background is a call to prayer; cowering in a corner is the feel of thick black gauze covering faces and bodies. Although difficult to see, faceless women are hidden away in every stroke of the brush.

No matter where I look upon the canvas, there is an endless desert, an ocean of sand where the sun rises and sets. In the midst of the desert there is peace like a river, even while brutality lurks nearby. There is war that runs red, a dark smear across all the other colors. Finally, there are the writers, the great painters upon the landscape. In the endless, timeless desert nights, prophets and poets write down ancient stories about life, love, and war with a passionate fury giving life to dead heroes.

I want to walk upright into the painting. Like Alice in Wonderland, I want to meet the characters, slide into the fantasy, run away in fear, and try to make some sense of it all. "Off with her head!" Oh, I hope not! Actually, I lived to tell the story; that's no small miracle.

This book is my painting -- black letter upon white parchment. I learned the motion and the rhythm in Baptist Sunday School when I was a small child in the South. There was something about falling walls of Jericho, sounds of trumpets, sonnets of Song of Solomon that was thrilling. The thrill became a religious pursuit of that hero of heroes, the historic Jesus. Interestingly, my pursuit led to a political study of geopolitics which led me straight into Judaism, Christianity, and Islam.

September 11, 2001 never surprised me, although it saddened me. New York and Washington, DC in mourning for all who died, our fallen heroes, was too sad to put into words. Its cause was our inability to see through the prism, to the darkness of death flickering through the beauty of bright blue skies. September 11, in my mind, was the Middle East exploding into the world once more. It happened in Europe in the 1970s, and in many other places since then. Why was America not more prepared? The answer is simple: we never saw it because we never saw it. It was right in front of our face, and we never saw it. I believe we must teach ourselves how to look through layers and see clearly with the eyes of an artist. There is a sound, a dance, a feel, a smell, a cry, a laughter that is "Middle East." Only when we understand and appreciate the Middle East, with all it nuances, will we be able to distinguish terrorists and know how to protect ourselves.

My book is my attempt to bring you, for a moment in time, into my painting. Enjoy it and take from it what you will!

UNVEILINGS
A Desert Journey
by
Patricia Adora Clark Taylor

FORWARD, *PART ONE*

GETTING TO RIYADH

Livorno, Italy -- 1973

CHET AND ME -- TOURING MONTE CARLO FROM ITALY -- 1975

Relocating to Italy

The flight from Baltimore, Maryland to New York to Rome was longer than I had anticipated. I was acquainted with long flights from California to Okinawa and the Pacific Rim where we lived for five years before moving to Maryland; but somehow, I didn't expect Rome to be so far away. Fortunately, Allen, our nine year old son, and Preston, his four year old brother, were good travelers. We previously lived in Okinawa, Japan, where Preston was born; the two boys practically grew up traveling on airplanes. My husband Chet, now relaxed and dozing, slept for most of the flight. He was happy to have the packing of household goods and all of the responsibilities of overseas moving removed from him. It had been a hectic move. We decided not to sell our house on the

Chesapeake Bay in Pasadena, Maryland, but to rent it instead. We painted and cleaned right up until the day of departure. We were exhausted!

My mind wondered back to this time a year ago when we traveled from Hawaii to Maryland in anticipation of "settling down" in Maryland for a few years. Strange how things rarely turn out the way we expect. Anyway, the year was now 1973, and I was thirty two years old. The past six years of my life had been a whirlwind of travel. My husband Chet Taylor, a civil engineer with the US Army Corps of Engineers, was rapidly gaining a reputation as an engineer of some merit who, along with his family, could adapt quickly to any place and any situation. Chet was becoming a trouble shooter of the first order as we moved to Cape Canaveral, Florida to build missile launching pads, to Okinawa to build runways at Kadena Air Base during the Viet Nam War, to Kwajalein in the Marshall Islands for underwater construction related to missile launchings from California's Vandenberg Air Base, to Hawaii, to Maryland, and now to Italy where the Corps of Engineer's Mediterranean Division was located near Livorno. I wondered about the toll extracted from our family life as we faced one move after another. But, never mind; for now, Italy was ahead of us, and I was excited about living at the seaside near Pisa, Livorno, and Florence!

I looked at our precious, beautiful boys. Nine year old Allen had the seat next to the window to get his own view of the world; but for now, he was sleeping, curled up with his pillow. Next to him, four year old Preston also was curled up, with his thumb securely in his mouth. On the other side of me, Chet slept with one leg jutted out into the aisle. As they rested peacefully, I had time to reflect on decisions we made during the past few months. Allen would spend the summer with us at our new home in the seaside Italian town of Tirrenia, located, near Pisa (with its famous leaning tower). At the end of the summer, Allen would travel to Florida to be with grandparents who would drive him to a private boarding school in Lake Wales, Florida. Allen, who was learning disabled, had difficulty in school; his disability was both visual and auditory. In the classroom, he often confused words and sounds, even though he generally was a bright, outgoing child. Extensive testing revealed Allen's need for teachers with special training who were successful in teaching students like Allen. The school was expensive; living and working in Italy, would help us afford the costs. Finally the plane touched down in Rome. It was good to get out and stretch, but I was disappointed that the airport looked old and dirty! I didn't realize it then, but within a few years, this airport would look good to me when I would fly in from my desert compound in Riyadh, Saudi Arabia.

Saudi Arabia Military Construction
Our connecting flight was a local flight from Rome to the small airport at Tirrenia, near Livorno, the location of Camp Darby and the Corps of Engineers' offices. Friends met us and escorted us to the seaside hotel where we would stay until finding a house. Several nights later we were in the lounge at the Officers' Club at Camp Darby. Some of the Corps engineers, all men, were sitting with us. These guys were seasoned world travelers who relocated from place to place, working military construction jobs. They were like hunting hounds that could get the "scent" of world events and know the next location for a military construction "build up". In the 1960's, events in Viet Nam, China, and Korea

signaled a need for military construction in the Far East. By the 1970s, they were focused on changing world events in the Middle East; some had relocated from Japan or Okinawa or Viet Nam to Italy, prepared to move into the Middle East. The discussion turned to Saudi Arabia and to planning for a huge military buildup.

Top right, me working with a Revlon customer in Naples; top left, Allen and Me; bottom, Preston with me as we watch a parade in Livorno.

1973 Arab Oil Embargo

That night in Italy, I thought about the evening's discussion regarding the next "exciting" horizon -- the Middle East and Saudi Arabia. I knew what the future held for me as certainly as I have ever known anything. Later, when Chet and I were alone, I declared, "No, I will not go to Saudi Arabia with you. I am willing to go many places, but Saudi Arabia is not one of those places!" A few months later, the 1973 Arab Oil Embargo left us with no oil for heating. Snow covered the ground. We burned pine cones in the fireplace for heat, but we were cold most of the time. Our Italian "gasolio" man was afraid to deliver oil to Americans because the Italians were rationing what little oil was available. Nevertheless, in the dead of a frozen night, he would deliver oil to us when possible so we could have heat. He simply said, "I remember World War II; the Americans were good people."

During the next three years, I was to recall the "Saudi" conversation over and over again.

In the course of those years, the world seemed to turn upside down as the word "oil" was used more and more in conversations about world economics and global power. The Mediterranean Division of the US Army Corps of Engineers became the Middle East Division; the Camp Darby offices divided their personnel between new offices in Virginia and Riyadh. Chet's work became centered in the very heart of the country where I refused to live. Chet had little choice with his work. He could relocate to the Virginia office or live and work in Riyadh. Either way, he would remain working in the Saudi program. Our special consideration was for Allen who was doing very well in the special education school in Florida. If we returned to the States, we would not be able to afford to keep him in the school. Overseas we were given housing and other benefits. So, in the summer of 1976, I found myself in the Rome Airport with Chet, Allen (who was home with us for the summer), and Preston. We arrived at the airport on a bus from Tirrenia filled with other Corps families loaded down with suitcases, boxes, caged animals, and children of all ages. We were traveling to a land that I despised, even though I had never been there. As a woman, I knew I would be handicapped. I would not be able to drive; I would be confined to our living quarters most of the time. My "Saudi plan" was to secure a job in order to have a Saudi driver, along with finances to return to Europe every three months for a few days for "time out". I had worked part-time for Revlon Cosmetics in Okinawa and in Italy; my Revlon supervisor had spoken with me about the possibility of my ordering products into Saudi Arabia, but I was making no commitments!

Italy: The Best World
It was difficult to leave Italy. Preston had it right; when we first arrived in Italy, he exclaimed, "This is the best world yet!" During three years of Italian life, I met new people and found new learning opportunities. I studied Italian language and took an art-history course. The beautiful Italian city of Florence became a familiar city with elegant works of art by Michelangelo and many other artists from ancient to modern. To this day, I love the tall buildings with their iron-gray facades and arched doorways. Heavy wooden doors guard entryways into massive rooms with high domed ceilings and marble floors. These splendid buildings housed some of the world's finest art. What fun it was to ride the train from Pisa or Livorno into Florence and spend the day shopping and viewing great works of art. In the afternoon, there would be time for a glass of wine and lunch at Mama Gina's restaurant located just blocks away from the Ponte Vecchio Bridge, lined with gold and silk and leather shops. Staying overnight at the Continental Hotel, located just at the foot of the Ponte Vecchio Bridge, was a special treat that Chet and I enjoyed on several occasions. Preston, also, had an ideal life. Now seven, he enjoyed his classes at Camp Darby, played "little league ball", and rode his bike throughout the small Italian community with his dog Julie chasing behind him. Now, Preston faced an unknown world.

JULIE AND PRESTON

While living in Italy, we traveled to Greece, Switzerland, Germany, and England. We spent a week in Athens touring museums and places of interest. We enjoyed Greek food and the colorful Bazuki dancers. We traveled to Venice and Pompeii, and we drove the breathtaking Amalfi drive along the Italian coast and visited Sorrento. We went by boat to the island of Elba, located off the coast of Italy, where Napoleon stayed for a time. We traveled north to Austria and Switzerland and Germany and saw breath-taking scenery of icy mountain peaks that plunged into lush green valleys. We flew to London to see Agathia Christie's long-running mystery play, "The Mouse Trap". We went to Buckingham Palace and saw the changing of the guards. Preston and Allen traveled with us during the summers. We always were happy to visit places of interest together. Sometimes Chet's parents flew to Rome where we met them and traveled together. It was a busy three years! Back in the States during these three years, my family was experiencing change. First, my sister Grace, who had been in the drug culture and studied numerous philosophies about life, was returning to her Christian faith. Her letters to me shone with excitement. Also, my dad had come into a strong relationship with God through Jesus Christ. Amazingly, alcohol, which had such a strong hold on his life, was gone from him forever.

I found the religious conversion a bit amazing; but considering that my dad's family, the Clark family, produced a long line of Methodist ministers beginning with John David Clark who came to Georgia from Scotland in the 1700s, it seemed plausible. I've always found my family to be a bit odd; my mother's father (it was whispered in family circles) was of European Jewish descent. When I asked my mother how we ended up attending the Baptist church when I was a child, she answered that she enjoyed going to the Baptist church in Birmingham, Alabama when she was a child and just kept going, embracing the teachings which were passed on to me. When I was just a child, she would tell me about the importance of the birth of Israel as a nation in Palestine. My mother is a life-long student of eschatology or "end-times" theory about the return of Jesus as the savior of the world. Between my father's ancestry and my mother's enthusiasm, how could I not be Christian? By the time I was ten years of age, my Sunday School teacher remarked to my mother that I could teach the class. The Old Testament and the New Testament were embedded in my brain. I already was weary of hearing about Paul's travels as written in the New Testament. Baptists are big on Paul's travels. I knew, even as a child, that I wanted to have my own traveling experiences and decide matters for myself. History was the hook that kept me deeply interested in Christianity. Someday, I wanted to travel to exotic places and see Biblical history with my own eyes.

Rome's Middle East Roots
At the same time Christianity was transforming my family, Italy directed my path towards the middle east. So much of Italy was about early Christianity which grew out of ancient middle east conflict. Determined to survive, the early Jesus movement attached itself to mother Rome. For three hundred years, Rome attempted to destroy the fledgling religion. The outcome was that Rome and Christianity became solidly linked together. Christianity identified with Rome and Rome identified with Christianity, resulting in the emergence of a great world religion infused with a sense of art, beauty, power, and democratic rule. Rome, which fought so mightily against this alien religion, finally embraced its enemy and became Christianity's great protector. Roman authority empowered Christian ideas. Working together, they produced some of the world's greatest art, especially during the Italian High Renaissance in the 15th Century which was the time of Michelangelo, Leonardo di Vinci, and others who pushed the limits of thought, reason, and creativity.

I had a deep interest in early European art history with its roots in Egyptian architecture and art. The Egyptian culture impacted early Greek art and culture, finally giving rise to the great Roman civilization with its massive roadways, archways, mighty Greek columns that evolved into Roman columns, and great buildings with creative use of stone and marble as seen in colorful mosaics and striking floor designs. The massive walls and floors were covered by huge arched ceilings pointing to the heavens and allowing streams of light to flood otherwise cold, dark rooms. Without realizing what was happening, I was drawn deeper and deeper into the root cultures responsible for Rome's transformation. (Even as a child, I knew that one day I would travel to the African continent and to Egypt to better understand ancient history. When I finally got there, I realized Egypt was largely a nation of Moslems. I had to "see it" to "see it.") In October of 1974, a year and four months after arriving in Italy, I took a three week "Holy Land" tour of the middle east which departed from Rome destined for Beirut, Jordan, Israel, and Egypt. Twenty-two Camp Darby adults made up our tour group. All of us were young enough to cover a lot of territory physically, while absorbing large amounts of information.

In the fall of 1974, during the three week tour of ancient sites, I was introduced to places and people who enabled me to see with greater understanding. I came face to face with Abraham of the Bible, who, several thousand years ago, lived in what is now Iraq; he relocated to Palestine which includes modern day Israel and Jordan. He moved out of Iraq's ancient city of Ur because God commanded him to, "Go." Four thousand years ago, Abraham relocated to the Jordan Valley, where he had two sons, Isaac (later known as Israel) and Ishmael. The sons fathered two great nations, the Arabs and the Jews. Two thousand years ago, Jesus, a Jewish teacher, became the Jewish link to non-Jews and provided a pathway back to the God of Abraham -- the same God who walked in the garden of Eden with Adam and Eve. That "way" is written in the New Testament of the

Bible. At the same time, I became sympathetic to the plight of Palestinians who were not Christian and who were deeply of the Islamic faith. For me, trying to reconcile the differences would take a number of years.

Overlapping Layers of Time: Ancient Sites Surrounded by Modern Conflict

To walk where Jesus walked is a unique experience! For me, it was life changing as my eyes quickly adapted from ancient history to modern-day conflict and back again to ancient history. Everywhere there were ancient sites colliding with modern warfare. I took notes from our guide the entire time we were in this area and later wrote to friends and family, hoping to make the experience come alive for them. At the time, they were viewing Christianity from American church traditions and teachings. I wanted to expand that experience into the reality of being "on site" to record a kind of "walking history." The letter became part of my own growing up experience. (I kept it all these years because it was a reference point, a starting place for a much longer journey that transformed me and helped me embrace other peoples, religions, and cultures.) During the trip, as planned, I recorded Christianity's early history; but I also developed an empathy with the plight of homeless Palestinians and began to take notice of another great religion known as Islam. In the coming years, my quest would take me deep into the heart of Saudi Arabia and Egypt, and I would travel to Israel to study conflict resolution and to witness war firsthand. My friends were to become the people of the lands stretching from Saudi Arabia across Israel and into Egypt.

My sister Grace was inspired by my letter of the middle east tour; a year later she visited Israel. Following is my letter, written in buses, climbing up stone steps, crowding into narrow alleyways, standing on historic sites. I wanted to know the truth about Jesus. Who was he really; and this small place on planet Earth known as Jerusalem, why was it so important to so many people? My trip was a search for the historic Jesus and for the mystery surrounding his birth and death; and I wanted to know more about the Arab world. Some of my Camp Darby friends were beginning to depart Italy for Riyadh. At the time of this Middle East tour, Chet and I had not yet made the decision to go to Riyadh.

OUR FAMILY IN ITALY -- PRESTON WITH HIS BIKE, CHET, ME, AL, AND CHET'S MOTHER

UNVEILINGS
A Desert Journey
by
Patricia Adora Clark Taylor

FORWARD, *PART TWO*

MIDDLE EAST PREVIEW
My Travels in Lebanon, Jordan, Israel, Egypt -- 1974

*Notes: 1970, **Palestinian Refugees** – In Lebanon, in the early 1970s, difficulties arose over the presence of Palestinian refugees, including Yasser Arafat and the Palestinian Liberation Organization (PLO). Many of the refugees arrived in Lebanon after the 1967 Arab-Israeli war and "Black September" hostilities in Jordan in 1970. At the same time in Lebanon, Muslin and Christian differences grew more intense*

*1975, **Lebanese Civil War** – Full-scale war broke out in Beirut in April 1975. After shots were fired at a church, gunmen in Christian East Beirut ambushed a busload of Palestinians. Palestinian forces joined Muslim factions as the fighting persisted, eventually spreading to most parts of the country.*

In 1974, I traveled in the Middle East at a time of conflict that would give rise to greater conflict in coming decades. For political reasons, no one was willing to come to the aid of Palestinian refugees. Eventually, the world would pay a high cost for such neglect of individuals in desperate need of help. The Biblical story of the Good Samaritan reminded me of the modern-day story of Palestinian (and other) refugees, except there was no kind traveler to offer aid and no good ending to the Palestinian story. There were only terrorized refugees with no hope. The camps became a lightening rod attracting dissidents and spawning ideas of revenge and revolution which later empowered Islamic revolution and gave birth to 21st century terrorism.

1974, My Letter from the Middle East to Family and Friends:
Wednesday, October 16, 1974 – Amman, Jordan

We are up and out early this morning. We are excited! This is the day we go to Jerusalem. So far into our trip, we spent two days in Beirut, a modern, exciting city that reminds me of Hong Kong. Beirut is a free port and a global market place. Our tour group had fun in Beirut's bazaar or "open air markets." The gold market was exciting, even it I could only look. I bought apples, delicious looking grapes, and a cantaloupe. I was with a couple of friends, and we took the fruit to our hotel, washed it and ate some for lunch. It was so good!

Baalbeck
We also took a tour around the area, and then drove an hour into the countryside to see Baalbeck, where Romans built colossal structure, producing a lasting monument to ancient gods. Those Romans, such mighty builders, went everywhere, much like the Corps of Engineers! We are told these building, beautifully preserved, are the largest and grandest buildings ever built by the Romans. Of monumental proportions, they tower high above the Beqaa plain, proclaiming Rome's power. Baalbeck, located on two main trade routes, is ancient city and worship site that refused to pass away. As our tour group examined and photographed this awesome place, our guide told us that we were near the village of one of Lebanon's famous poets, Kilhil Gibran. He said with pride, "He is our prophet." The drive back into the city was a time of reflection about the intertwining of ancient and modern cultures. That evening in Beirut, we ate dinner at an open air, seaside restaurant with large archways and stone floors. A soft breeze surrounded us that

evening. Beirut was an incredibly beautiful city!

Palestinian Camps

The next day we visited Palestinian camps, located in Beirut. The Palestinian refugees, who relocated after war with Israel, were left on display by wealthy Arab nations who refused to assist them and a world that ignored them. The camps, stretched out along city streets, were an eyesore on the world and a political nightmare; no one was willing to meet the needs of these poor people who lived in a world of rejection. I witnessed a large section of the city where they lived in whatever makeshift dwellings they could create – along sidewalks, in parks, or wherever they could exist. As I viewed the camps, it occurred to me that, one day, the world would face the wrath of these Palestinian children. That night, several of us were walking back to our hotel after dinner. It was another soft October night in Beirut. Suddenly we heard gunfire nearby; then we herd it again and again. As we ran to the Phoenician Hotel where we stayed for two nights, we saw tanks in the street next to the hotel. A civil war loomed on the horizon. As I write this, it is difficult for me to believe that tanks are in the street in Beirut, and the world does not care. It occurs to me that the world is in love with war. It has become the acceptable sacrificial rite of killings off the world's youth to please the unquenchable appetite of ancient pagan gods and modern arms dealers.

Amman, Jordan

After visiting Beirut, we flew to Jordan to the capitol city of Amman. It is obvious that we are in a "hot spot." Everywhere on this trip our luggage is inspected, and we are searched. I am glad we are on a well-organized tour; otherwise, we would be held up for hours being searched and questioned. Nevertheless, Amman proved to be fun and interesting. The hotel was modern and new. Construction is under way all over the city of Amman. King Hussein is revered; it is on wonder. He takes great pride in his country, and it is beginning to show. Our guide is proud that King Hussein is friends with the U.S. He tells us that King Hussein was the first foreign dignitary to visit President Ford at the White House.

The Bedouin

It was interesting to tour areas near Amman. On our way to an old caravan city, we came upon a Bedouin tribe taking their camels to a water hole. We got off the bus, mixed among the Bedouin, and took pictures. One of the men wanted his picture taken. Another was angry because his picture was taken; he believed his soul would be stolen with the photograph. There seemed to be a hundred camels. Such tribes roam the desert with camels, just as they have done for a thousand years or more. I am told that some Bedouin live for a hundred years! They seem peaceful, proud, and happy. They are such a colorful group with their brownish camels with huge eyelashes weighted down with large, course red-carpet saddle-bags; huge carpet and blanket rolls; and beads and trinkets of all sorts. Their life is simple; they are known for their hospitality and generosity. With them are their sheep, goats, donkeys, and horses. The desert is their classroom. They know every kind of herb which they use for food and medicine. Their map is the bright desert sky, from which they chart their course. The desert, with its oceans of sand dunes, rocky plains, and mountain wilderness, is where they live and die. They are mysterious, lively, energetic, thoughtful, and poetic.

Petra

We continued our trip to the historic caravan city of Petra mentioned in the Bible in the Old Testament. Petra was established over two thousand years ago by Nabataean Arabs, a nomadic tribe who began a commercial empire extending to Syria. However, the site must have been well-known by travelers even before that time. Petra is a breath-taking, rose-red city carved out of sandstone. The ancient city, surrounding an open valley, is located in the heart of desert mountains near an ancient trade route. The formal entrance is through the Sic which is a narrow entrance winding and twisting through sandstone mountains rising high above the rocky terrain.

Our bus is parked on the side of the highway. All we see are deserted mountains and about twenty-five horses with several smiling Arab guides on horseback awaiting our arrival. We mount up, enter the Sic and ride into the now-deserted city. Straight up, on either side of me, are tall mountains so close that I can touch them, stretching higher and higher into blue sky. There is no sound in the quiet desert. We are in awe as we ride speechless through the sandstone mountains. In some places, the sunlight is hidden by the great mountains. The sky is blue without a cloud. Suddenly, we hear the thundering sound of hoofs pounding the desert floor. We hear the group of Arab men before we see them. They are riding powerful horses toward us as if to greet us. The men, with their headdresses flying in the wind, come seemingly from nowhere. They are laughing, waving, and riding their horses past us, kicking up dust all around! As suddenly as they appear, they are gone. What a breath-taking moment!

My first glimpse of Petra reveals ornate pillars jutting out from the mountain surface. It is a carved city, to beautiful to describe, still attached to its mother stone. Like the sculptor, Michelangelo, who envisioned arms, heads, finger, and toes stuck in the marble stone just waiting to be unleashed, the Petra builders were artists who envisioned a city in a mountain; they chiseled, cut, and delicately carved their way through layers of color to redefine the mountain. Once inside the ancient city, we dismount and climb up the walls into cave-like parts of the city. From here we can see why we came on horseback; the city is circular with only one narrow entryway to be seen. Everywhere we look, the carved city reveals sandstone layers with rainbow colors. Apparently, the Nabataeans built their city here because of the uniquely beautiful sandstone that also would have been suitable for rock carving. The sandstone is layered in colors of yellow, orange, brown, white, red, grey, pink, and mauve. It is an awesome sight! Back at our bus, we dismount and bid farewell to our horses and our guides.

Dead Sea Valley

But those events happened yesterday. Today I am leaving Amman and going to Jerusalem where we will stay for several days! This morning our tour group, leaving Amman, saw King Hussein's palace, soon afterwards we saw an "embassy row" of new, modern homes for dignitaries. All of the sites were impressive. Now we are traveling in the bus, and I see Mount Nebo in the distance where Moses looked over into the "promised land." We are told it is the highest mountain on this range. Now we are descending below sea level down into the Jordan Valley. Everywhere it is rocky and barren. On the horizon, I barely make out Jericho to my right and the Dead Sea to my left. Somewhere in this area might have been the location of Sodom and Gomorra. In the desert near us, we saw black, porous rock which covers the desert for miles. Might it have been from an asteroid or a volcano thousands of years ago? Now we are in the area of the Jordan Valley. It is a fertile area with bananas, lemons, oranges, fruits, and vegetables of various kinds.

We are in the Dead Sea Rift Valley which extends the length of Jordan and defines Jordan's western border with Israel. The land-locked Dead Sea originally was formed over five million years ago and is the deepest part of the Dead Sea Rift. Its water is dense with salt, giving buoyancy to swimmers who float with ease. The salty sea is thought to have healing properties; people come from around the world to bathe in its waters, to soak up the sun, and breathe the air. Formed from ancient earthquakes and volcanoes throughout the region, the Dead Sea's surface lies deep below sea level. We are told that earthquakes have caused repeated destruction within the valley; an earthquake might have been responsible for the destruction of Sodom and Gomorrah as told in the Bible. Since the war of 1967, the valley is divided between Israel and Jordan. Israel has a large area of the valley, and Jordan gets some fruits and vegetables from Israel. Barren mountains are on either side of the fertile valley. We just passed a group of square-shaped clay or stone houses with flat roofs. It looks like a picture right out to the Old Testament. Now we are in a small village area. A Mercedes passes us on the dusty road. On the other side of the road, I see a little boy drinking a bottle of soda, a woman carrying a water bucket on her shoulder, and an old man on a donkey. Suddenly, in the distance, I can see the mountains of Jerusalem.

Checkpoints Along the Way
Now we are at a checkpoint. To my right is a vacant village. It looks bombed out. We are stopping at a small square-shaped house. Our tour guide is checking our passports with the guard. Our bus driver, a Palestinian living in Jordan just told us that he would like to go with us into Jerusalem. His family is there since 1967. He has a wife, brothers, and a grown daughter with children in Jericho, a city which we can see from here. He says, "Like Jerusalem, Jericho is so close and yet so far." His family comes to see him sometimes for a month at a time. He says, "Many people like me were caught with the forces after the war. My family had to stay behind. I was born and raised on this land. I will return soon to live, with or without the help of the U.S." I told him I thought Jerusalem, at least, should be a place where all people could visit freely; the city is sacred to so many people. He replied that because of the Jews, many people have been driven from their homes. "Until 1948 there was room for everyone. Then some land was given to Israel and now they want all Jews to come here and live. There is not enough room; they will want Jordan and other countries. But we will return one day."

Now we are at the second checkpoint which is the Allenby Bridge or the King Hussein Bridge. It is a small wooden bridge over a stream of water. I somehow expected more of the Jordan River. On the other side of the river, I can barely make out a blue and white flag; I think with a star.

Changing Buses and Bus Drivers
We have crossed the bridge ad changed buses. Our Palestinian driver could come no further. Now we are on an Israeli bus with an Israeli bus driver and we have gone only a short way to our first Israeli checkpoint. We are in a barren looking place. A small three room structure serves as a check-in area. To my left, I see a wire fence enclosure, behind which are Arab people; I think they are checking through to either enter Israel or return to Jordan. Our luggage is being removed from the bus; it will be opened and inspected. Now we are sitting on a wood bench inside a waiting room. The walls and floor are bare. My tour group is busy writing post cards. Other travelers are in the room; another tour group just joined us. I see two women knitting; one woman is doing needlepoint. I believe one couple is Quaker because the American looking woman is wearing a long print dress, a white bonnet, black stocking, and black shoes.

I just spoke with an Israeli man, about thirty-five, who works with a tour agency and is waiting to meet his tour group arriving from Jordan. He asked me about Jordan. I told him that Jordan and Lebanon were beautiful countries. I was eating an apple, and I told him it was from Lebanon. He said he hoped to see Lebanon one day; he knew about Lebanon's wonderful fruit. He was positive about getting to Lebanon one day.

Anis, Our Tour Guide
We are back on our tour bus; our new tour guide has just introduced himself. His name is Anis. He is telling us that we are going through the plains of Gilgal where the Israelites camped after being with Moses and coming down from the Moab mountains behind us. We are headed for Jericho. Anis says that the location where we just crossed the Jordan River is near where Jesus was baptized and where Elisha was taken into heaven.

It is a hot, sunny day without a cloud in the blue sky. We are approaching a small village where date palms line the street. Arabs are shopping in narrow shops displaying fruit and vegetable stands outside. We are passing four Israeli soldiers with machine guns. We are coming to a village of small, square, clay homes. Further ahead, I see soldiers and tanks at another checkpoint.

Dead Sea and Qumran
We are coming to the area of the Dead Sea Scrolls. Anis relates a story about the scrolls. He says they were put into caves about 66 AD. A religious sect, the "Essenes," lived in the rocky desert wilderness and devoted themselves to living a pure life and to copying accurately the books of the Old Testament. It is believed by some that John the Baptist was a member of the Essenes. In 1947, their scrolls were found by a shepherd who was looking for a lost sheep in a place identified as Qumran. Because sheep often get lost in caves, the shepard threw a stone into the cave and heard a strange sound. He looked into the cave and found clay jars containing scrolls with Jewish writing. The shepard took them to an antique dealer, who, in turn, wanted to get rid of them. In 1947 it was dangerous to have anything Jewish in this Palestinian region. The scrolls from the Qumran caves were sold to a buyer for a few dollars. The buyer sent photographs to Chicago University experts, who realized the value of the scrolls. Since then, there has

been much excitement about the scrolls and many excavations in this area.

Now we are at the lowest point on earth. It is so hot! 110 degrees! All around are barren rocks and hills. To me, it is a place without life, except for our little group. We seem to be standing n the middle of nowhere. To one side are mountains, and on the other side, in the far distance, is the Dead Sea. It is blue, beautiful, and ever so still. There is an oppressive feeling. It seems hard to breathe, and it is so very, very dry. It was the dryness that helped preserve the scrolls. The files stick to us and refuse to fly away. This is an eerie place. Qumran dates back to 800 BC, the time of Judea. Our guide says the Essenes abandoned Qumran because King Herod forced them out in 37 BC. The area, conquered by the Romans, was later deserted by them.

The Dead Sea also is referred to as the Sea of Lot and the Eastern Sea. Some historians believe that Sodom and Gomorrah are buried under the sea. No life lives in the sea; and at one time in history, deadly gasses arose from it. There are stories of birds flying over and dropping dead out of the sky. We are told that the sea is thirty-five miles wide and for-eight miles long. It is about one third salt and is oily and bitter. The sea is surrounded by the Moab Mountains, the Sinai Desert, Sea of Galilee, and Judea. Anis explains that today, modern Sodom, at the south of the Dead Sea, is the lowest point on earth. There is a theory that ancient Sodom and Gomorrah might have been destroyed by explosions in this area. The exact location of the Biblical cities is unknown, although it is believe that modern Sodom lies in the vicinity of the ancient site. Now we are back in the bus traveling through the valley of Gilgal on our way to Jericho. The Israelites camped here; and Saul was anointed king here. Suddenly, we are at another checkpoint with soldiers holding machine guns and two-way radios.

Jericho
After passing through the checkpoint, we arrived in Jericho and had lunch consisting of tomato and cucumber salad, broiled chicken, and Syrian bread with eggplant dip. I had a beer that was $1.50. Most likely that was more than the whole! I will not make that mistake again. We traveled on to an excavation site; Anis tells us it is the ancient site of Jericho. The site penetrates the earth for twenty civilizations. We are in one of the oldest inhabited spots known on earth. The destruction of Jericho was in 1400 BC. Archeologists dispute what caused it, perhaps thousands of footsteps marching in unison and blowing trumpets? Here I am reminded of James Mitchner's novel, The Source., about an archeological site extending deep into the earth and revealing ancient stories of the people and their culture. From where I am standing, I can see an excavated area, known as a tell, with mud brick walls. Fire rings can be seen at certain levels, so it is believed that the city was destroyed by fire at one time. Down about sixty-five feet is the base of a watchtower. A staircase is inside the tower; two human skeletons have been found here which carbon date to 8,000 BC. Standing at the top of this tell, I can look over parts of Jericho as it is today. This is the sight that Moses would have seen from Mt. Nebo. I am looking at a lush green valley lined with date palms. The climate is subtropical and hot!

Now we are back on the bus and are going up, up, up to Jerusalem where we will stay in a hotel during our Israel visit. We are penetrating the wilderness of Judea with its dry, desolate, desert terrain. In the distance, I see shepards with sheep on rocky hills. I wonder how they survive; it is so hot! I can understand why feet washing was a gracious custom at the time of Jesus. In this 100 degree weather, I would enjoy having my feet washed in cold water. Suddenly, I am back in the 20th century. Tanks are all along the road at intervals. I guess Jews and Arabs will never stop fighting without a miracle.

Anis is telling us that, in Bible times, it was a two-day walking trip from Jericho to Jerusalem. When Jesus told the "good Samaritan story", he was speaking about this area. In the story, a man is beaten by thieves and left to die. People pass him by and do not help him. Finally a "good Samaritan" takes the dying man to an inn and pays for his stay and his healing. Anis expounds on this story. He see Jericho being the Garden of Eden; Adam left the garden and was bruised and hurt as he journeyed upward. A man (Jesus) came to save h him and to care for him and promised the innkeeper that he would pay more, if required, on his way back (which Anis sees as Jesus' "Second Coming" to save the earth from destruction and to save his people.)

Bethany
We are entering the town of Bethany, home of Mary and Martha where Jesus brought their dead brother Lazarus to life. We stop at an excavated church behind which are further excavations. Anis explains that, after the death of Jesus, Byzantine churches were built over ancient holy sites. In modern times, the first excavation by archeologists is to find a Byzantine church; another excavation is for the site under the church. Excavations here unearthed a Byzantine church and the, under the church, a home with a courtyard with beautiful mosaic floors. Some believe this is the home of Lazarus, Mary, and Martha. While I am standing in this spot thinking of Lazarus emerging from the dead, a loud call to prayer for the Moslems comes from loudspeakers of nearby mosques. It is the end of Ramadan, a month long Moslem religious holiday. Ramadan is a time of fasting from sun up until sun down; now the fasting ends.

Garden of Gethsemane
We are approaching the famous city walls of Jerusalem which can be seen on one side of the highway. On the other side of the highway is the prominent Church of All Nations, located at the Garden of Gethsemane. The word Gethsemane means "oil press." In this area, a follower probably owned an oil press with an olive garden. We are touring this site. The olive trees in the garden are huge with large twisted trunks and knotty places that look half eaten away. We are told the olive trees are roughly 2,000 years old and are known as the "Witness Trees" because, as young shoots, they would have witnessed the agony of Jesus as he prayed in the garden. According to our guide, olive trees are the only trees that survived the flood. When Noah sent the dove out, it returned with an olive branch which now has become a peace symbol.

Bethlehem
Now we are driving up, up, up the slopes of Mount Zion and are arriving at a main street where we pass military trucks and tanks. We continue upward to a small hillside town known as Bethlehem. Three hundred and thirty years after the time of Jesus, King

Constantine ordered a church built over the cave believed to be the birthplace of Jesus. Today the church has been excavated and underneath is a cave. Is it really the place? We are told that caves were used for stables. Leaving the site, we see down into the green, rolling hills of the Fields of Boaz, which are the same fields where the shepherds were watching their flocks of sheep at night and saw a bright star shinning over the stable where Jesus was born. We have stopped, and I am looking out over these fields. It is a peaceful moment; the long day is coming to a close.

Thursday, October 17, 1974 – Jerusalem and Surrounding Area

Suddenly I awake early the next morning. It is Thursday; today we head north from Jerusalem, and there is much to see and explore. Anis explains that David conquered Jerusalem in 1,000BC and made it the capitol of his kingdom. Now we pass the village Nob where David fled from King Saul. King Saul's palace was located just outside the city of Jerusalem. To the left is the Hill of Joy where Samuel judged his people. We are on the road to Damascus which was traveled by the apostle Paul. Now we are in Ramah, the birthplace of Samuel. Now we are on the outskirts of the valley of Gibeon. Along this road, Jesus appeared to his disciples after his resurrection. Now we are into the Valley of Mespah where Saul was anointed by Samuel. Now we are in Beeroth, a day's walking journey from Jerusalem. Here Mary and Joseph realized, after a day of walking and celebrating with friends, that Jesus was not with them and turned back to Jerusalem to find him. To our right is the small mountain chain of Luz where God appeared to Abraham and said he would give him this land. Lot and his brother Abraham looked out over the region below and chose their land. I am thinking that so much history and so many stories are packed into one small area of planet Earth!

Kingdom of Israel

We are leaving the southern kingdom of Judah and entering the northern kingdom of Israel. After the death of Solomon, the tribes became divided; ten of the tribes comprised the northern kingdom of Israel. Two tribes comprised the southern kingdom of Judah. Assyria defeated the ten northern tries in 721 BC; the nation of Israel was deported and scattered throughout the Middle East. Some probably married outside of Israel and eventually lost their Jewish identity. While Anis weaves his stories of time past, I am watching people walking along the roadside. I notice two girls with dark slacks and brightly colored blouses. They are carrying jars on their heads or on their shoulders; they have great posture!

As we ride along in the bus, Anis stands in front and speaks with us, answering our many questions. Anis relates that he often guides groups of elderly people fulfilling a lifetime dream to see the Holy Land before they die. In contrast, he likes the youthfulness and energy of our group; and he responds with enthusiasm. He tells us he was born and raised near Jerusalem. He is Jewish and is a Christian of the Greek Orthodox faith. During his growing up years, his mother taught him much of the Bible by taking him to religious sites and relating ancient Bible stories. The stories are alive for Anis, and he makes them live for us. Now he is talking about Mount Hermon, which commands a view of Lebanon, Syria, and the area of Palestine and Israel. Anis believes that Mount Hermon is where Jesus was taken spiritually for the time of his temptation because, from that place, he would have an expansive view of powerful kingdoms.

Shiloh
Once more, we are in a discussion about Byzantine churches which began being built about three hundred years after the death of Jesus; they were built over sacred sites and have been clues in modern times to religious site locations. Our tour group seems fascinated by this revelation. The conversation changes as we approach Shiloh were the Arc of the Covenant remained for three hundred years before being taken by Philistines. Shiloh was the capitol of the Jewish tribes before David made Jerusalem the capitol. Solomon built a new temple at Jerusalem for the Arc of the Covenant; this temple site is located where the Moslem "Dome of the Rock Mosque" stands today. Also in Shiloh, Samuel was raised by Eli the priest.

Anis is telling us his Adam and Eve theory. He believes the Garden of Eden was in Palestine. Adam and Eve were expelled east to Mesopotamia, which means "between two rivers." He believes that civilization began between the Tigris and Euphrates rivers which would be in modern day Iraq. He believes the "sword of fire" used by God to separate Adam and Eve from Eden is the desert of Saudi Arabia. Anis tells us, however, that God always brings his prophets back to the land of Palestine, to Israel. Anis believes Jesus will return one day as a great world ruler and reign from Jerusalem. I am reminded of Hal Lindsey's best seller, The Late, Great Planet Earth.

Jacob's Well
When Jesus lived in this area, there were three Roman districts known as Galilee, Samaria, and Judea. We are entering the land of Efram; in the time of Jesus, it was known as Samaria. Jesus passed through her on his way to Galilee. We have arrived at the Biblical Sichem, of great spiritual importance because Jacob, Isaac, and Esau lived here at different times. We get out of the bus and sit under shade trees around Jacob's Well while Anis reveals more about this site. Here, about 2,000 years ago, during the noon hour, Jesus first revealed himself as the Messiah. He gave this revelation to a woman of bad reputation. Anis says the woman came to the well to draw water at the hottest time of the day when no one else would be there. She was a Samaritan, a sect of Jews who broke away from other Jewish tribes over the building location of the temple in Jerusalem. She was surprised that Jesus, a Jew, even spoke to her. Jesus conversed with her, relating incidents about her past. She was shocked that Jesus could know these things. Finally, he said to her, referring to the long-awaited Messiah, "I, who speak to you, am He." The story is told in the forth chapter of the book of John in the Bible.

Valley of Armageddon
We are back on the bus and are coming into Dothan where Joseph was sold into slavery by his brothers. This area has been excavated back to 87 BC. Saul was struck blind here. Near here, Jesus healed the lepers. Now we are coming to a huge, panoramic valley. This is the valley of Jezreel, otherwise known as the Valley of Armageddon. Twenty-eight battles have been fought here in different eras. Three continents come together here: Africa, Asia, and Europe. This is the crossroads of the world. The Kings Highway intersects here with another main highway. Historically, this has been both a prominent

trade area and a place of war.

In the background is Mount Carmel where Elisha called on God to prove himself to priests of Baal; God responded by sending fire from heaven. In ancient times, the worship of Baal permeated the Middle East. The golden calf was the symbol of Baal. The followers of Baal believed that Baal gave light, warmth, rain, humidity, fertility, and that he gave the world the gift of love. Even the Hebrews had to renounce Baal and worship Jehovah. Anis reminds us that while Moses was on the mountain top getting God's Ten Commandments; the people below were building a golden calf. The worship of Baal flourished even into the time of the Roman Empire. I am reminded that in Lebanon, we visited Baalbeck which means, "the city of Baal," where Roman architects and engineers created some of their tallest columns and boldest structures to build their great temples at Baalbeck.

Golan Height, Mount Hermon, Sea of Galilee.
We are passing a kibbutz which is a framing community inhabited mostly by immigrant Jews. The communal life enables them to share responsibilities and spend most of their time farming and building their community. Into the distance I see Mount Tabor where some believe Jesus transfigured into heaven. Anis believes it was Mount Hermon instead because the city, Caesarea Philippi, where Jesus was seen just before his transformation is at the base of Mount Hermon. Now we are coming into Galilee. I can see the Golan Heights which meet with Mount Hermon and where the border of Lebanon and Syria come together. The mountaintops of the Golan Heights are lush and green. I can just make out Mount Hermon in the far north. We are standing at the side of the road overlooking the Galilee area with the sea and mountains in the background. What a powerful moment in my life and what a beautiful view. I must pinch myself to believe it is all real!

Galilee and the Jordan River
The valley of Galilee is green and beautiful. The lake is deep blue surrounded by farmlands. Anis tell us that Moses would have seen this region from the desert mountain; he says this is the "real" land of Caanan. We have driven to an area of the Jordan River which empties into the Sea of Galilee. We stopped and got out to wade at the river's edge. The water is clear and cool and surrounded by green trees. Nearby, just stepping out of a sleek limousine, is an older couple with a Greek Arch Bishop with a very long beard… We watch as he walks into the water with the couple and baptizes them. He is still standing in the river and beacons to us. Two of our group wade into the river to him, and he baptizes them. Then I wade in and sit on a large rock in the river. The Arch Bishop dips a long leafy branch into the water and brings it up over my head several times while saying words that I could not hear because the water was pouring over me and splashing all around me. Then I kissed the cross which was around his neck. It was over in a moment, and I was stunned that it ever happened. We waded out of the water and the Arch Bishop gave me his card. The card reads: Theodossius Arch Bishop; Greek Covent; Bethany, Mary and Martha's House; P.O.B. 19121, Israel.

Back on the bus, I remained stunned by the baptism incident; it was so unexpected. I hear Anis announcing that we are leaving Tiberius, a Gentile city, which existed at the time of Jesus. We are going toward Capernaum where Jesus ministered and lived during much of his ministry. We are near Magdala, the home of Mary Magdalene. Mush of Jesus's ministry was here in this area. Here he called the fishermen to be "fishers of men." Here he changed a few fish and loaves into food for multitudes. We are at Peter's village which now lies in ruins and is the location of a large banana grove; the dense growth here reminds me of Hawaii. Behind Peter's village there is a panoramic view of green hillsides leading down to the blue Galilean sea. On these hills, Jesus, the great storyteller, taught the people a way of life that has survived two thousand years and that is recorded as the Beatitudes in the Bible. We leave this peaceful place and ride by a cliff that plunges down into the sea. Anis tells us this is where Jesus cast the demons into the herd of swine and the swine perished down into the sea below.

Now we are entering Capernaum where there is excavation of ruins. Jesus spent time in Capernaum because highways of the world connect here; caravans passed through here from all of the then known world. Here travelers met Jesus who took his message to foreign lands. People who were ill came here for the healing waters of nearby hot mineral springs; some came to Jesus to be healed. "Far Naum" is the real name of Capernaum, named for Naum, the last prophet of the Old Testament who is buried here.

Anis is telling us about his crossing the Sea of Galilee many times in a boat. He has been caught in a number of storms because winds come up fast without warning on an otherwise beautiful day, making it difficult to get to shore. Anis, frightened by the storms, says he would remember how Jesus slept in the boat and calmed the sea. Suddenly the subject changes. One of our group wants to know more about the Bedouin. Anis relates that they are descendants of Ishmael, the son of Abraham and Hagar. He says they have lived the same for thousands of years. Now we are coming into Cana of Galilee where Jesus performed his first miracle at the request of his mother. He and his mother were at a wedding when the host ran out of wine; his mother asked him to turn water into wine. He replied that his (of revelation) had not yet come; nevertheless, he did as she asked of him. Perhaps he dreaded his future.

Nazareth
I have seen such beautiful scenery today. Lunch was at a waterfront restaurant beside the Sea of Galilee where we had St. Peter's fish. In the afternoon, we went to Nazareth, located on a hill with a sweeping view of the valley below. The site we visited has been excavated to 300 BC. Below the ruins and down another fifty feet are ruins of a stone house built over a cave believed by some to have been the home of Mary, Joseph, and Jesus. We were told that it was normal in those days to build homes over caves so people would have a cool place in the summertime. Leaving Nazareth, I see much construction and new homes being built. We proceeded down, down the winding road to the Valley of Armageddon. Once more, I am surprised at the vastness of it. Anis tells us that the valley is sixteen miles long and twelve miles wide. Jesus must have been very familiar with this view which is so close to his home. Now it is dusk. There is one star in the clear sky as we ride through green rolling hills on our way back to Jerusalem. I am peaceful. I keep thinking how much mother would have enjoyed this.

Friday, October 18, 1974 – Jerusalem and Surrounding Areas
Mount of Olives

It is Friday. We are going from Jerusalem to the Mount of Olives and to Mount Zion. We are passing the ancient Flock Gate where Arabs are buying and selling and bartering their sheep, just as they have done for thousands of years. We can see the Kedron Valley; now we are crossing the valley and ascending the slope of the Mount of Olives. When we reach the top, I can see the Dead Sea and the Moab Mountains in the far distance; Anis says it is twenty-eight miles as the crow flies. To my right, I see the Gate Beautiful and the area of Solomon's Temple. Standing on the summit of the Mount of Olives, I can see all of Jerusalem below, including where Jesus traversed in his final hours when Pilot sent Jesus to religious leaders who proclaimed his death sentence.

Anis tells us that the population of Jerusalem at the time of Jesus was 50,000; but at Passover it swelled to maybe ten times that number. Where were they accommodated? They camped on surrounding hills. Some came a month ahead to camp on the Mount of Olives to get a good view of the city below. The Romans allotted various locations surrounding Jerusalem to various districts. Mount of Olives was designated for Galileans. Jesus spent the last year of his ministry in Jerusalem, mostly teaching in the temple. But he never spent a night within the city walls. The Mount of Olives became a favorite spot for Jesus and his disciples. Probably he spent many nights here where, as a Galilean, he would not be harmed by people from other districts. Here he recited the Lord's Prayer for the second time to his disciples, the first time was at the Sermon on the Mount. After his resurrection, Jesus appeared to his disciples on the Mount of Olives.

It is a quiet moment; our guide is reciting the Lord's Prayer in Aramaic, an Arabic dialect close to the language of Jesus. We are in a church which opens onto a garden. On the surrounding walls are mosaics displaying the Lord's Prayer in sixty-three languages.

Mount Zion

We are on our way to Mount Zion. We arrive at an excavation site, just outside the city walls. Anis says this is a sacred spot to the Jews because of an excavated sealed tomb below which has never been opened; the Jews believe it is the tomb of King David. Anis believes the Jews are afraid to open the tomb for fear they will not find anything! He has traversed this area many times and knows that an underground passageway leads from here, down the slopes, and into the city walls. Anis believes that King David is buried somewhere inside the city walls; and that, what is actually inside the tomb, is the long lost Arc of the Covenant. Anis, who has walked the passageway from the city to the tomb, says it is likely that elderly priests would have escaped to this place with the Arc when they were escaping from the enemy during the destruction of the city. We are allowed to go down inside the excavated area and see the tomb. It makes me wish that someone would open it. It seems to be sealed with a large stone. Anis explains that the Arc of the Covenant is a large container which houses the Ten Commandments given to Moses. There is a story about this tomb that, during excavation in the twelfth century, one of the men began to open the tomb. Suddenly, a voice came out saying, "A man is not yet to know." The terrified people sealed it; it has remained sealed since!

A dwelling, believed to have been the home of a rich man, was built over the tomb area; and a large room with Roman columns has been reconstructed to resemble the room of the Last Supper. It is believed that Jesus came to this area for the Last Supper and met his disciples here. In the Bible, Mark, chapter 14 tells us that the servant of the rich man who owned the house met the disciples and led them to his master's house. While we are standing in the room, Anis explains the last supper was not the Passover meal. Instead, it was the Hegera meal which is before the Passover. Jesus knew that he would not be with his disciples for Passover. Jewish religious leaders wanted him dead before Passover. Later Jesus was taken to Calvary and crucified between two thieves who, most likely, had been there for some time. Anis explains that crucifixion is a slow death and could take as long as eight days. The heart has to work harder and harder to cause the blood to be pumped back to the upper part of the body. The legs of the thieves were broken to cause internal bleeding and hasten death. The same was to have been done with Jesus, but he died quickly.

Shrine of the Book
Afterwards, we pass Israeli Parliament and Hebrew University where we see a large bronze statue of a Jewish candlestick known as a menorah which was given to Israel in 1948. Nearby is a small village where it is believed that Elizabeth, the mother of John the Baptist, lived and where Mary, the mother of Jesus, visited Elizabeth. Finally, we are at the museum known as the Shrine of the Book where the Dead Sea Scrolls, found by the shepherd boy at Qumran, are housed. The architecture is in black and white (a black wall is contrasted with the white dome of the structure.) The guide explains this is because the scrolls refer to the "sons of light and the sons of darkness." Inside we see the scrolls on display securely behind glass, and we even see how the pages were sewn together in ancient times. We also view artifacts found with the scrolls. We are told that the importance of the scrolls is that they record much of the Biblical text as it is recorded today. It is considered to be another proof of the authenticity of the scriptures. It occurs to me that the once dead scrolls have taken on a modern life of their own!

Mount Moriah – A Most Sacred Rock
Now we are inside Jerusalem's city wall near the Wailing Wall. We were searched twice by Israeli guards who fear that someone will deface the area. We are at the exquisite mosque known as the Dome of the Rock. Inside the Dome of the Rock is the threshing rock. (Interestingly, we also are near the site of King Solomon's temple, no longer in existence.) The rock is a huge flat rock which, after Abraham's time, became a threshing rock where people threshed wheat by stomping on it. According to our guide, this is the most sacred spot in all of Jerusalem for all three religions – Judaism, Christianity, and Islam. Here, Abraham brought Isaac to be sacrificed as proof that he believed in the one God.

Anis tells us that this sacred spot is first mentioned in the Bible when Abraham brings Isaac to be sacrificed; later it was the threshing rock. About 1,000 BC, David saw an angel over the rock in a dream and later he raised an alter over the threshing rock. David wanted to build a temple at this spot, but God would not allow him to build it because David, as a man of war, had killed others. However, God let Solomon build the temple at the height of the Jewish reign. Later, Nebuchadnezzar destroyed the Jewish temple; and the Arc of the covenant was lost. During 55 BC to 10 BC, Herod had the Jewish temple rebuilt to please the Jews. Jesus came to the temple as a child, and later as a Jewish rabbi or teacher. In 70 AD, the Jews were dispersed; the few who remained were not allowed back inside the city.

Jews at the Wailing Wall

They only could come to this wall and repeat their lamentations, wailing at the wall. During the Arab-Israeli war in 1967, Jews captured and entered all of Jerusalem for the first time since the dispersion.

Islam and the Dome of the Rock

Roughly 600 years after the death of Jesus, the religion of Islam came into existence. The Jews and Christians had a "sacred book," so Mohammed wrote an inspired book, the Koran, for the Arab nation. The Koran follows loosely some of the stories and teachings of the Bible, but actually is quite different from the Bible. According to Anis, Moslems believe that, in 636 AD, after Mohammed ascended into heaven, his follower Omar wanted a place for Moslems to worship; Omar chose this sacred spot. It was believed that Mohammed flew here from Mecca on a horse and prayed before being taken up into heaven.

Dome of the Rock

So in 691 BC, the Dome of the Rock was built. It is the earliest Arab architecture in the country; some consider it to be one of the Seven Wonders of the World. Its beauty is indescribable! From a distance, it looks to be a large pale blue octagon shaped structure with a gold dome. Actually, we are told, the dome is covered in guilted aluminum which was added in modern times. The upkeep of the mosque is a continuing project headed by King Hussein who collects money from Arab countries. As we continue our discussion, Anis tells us that "Moslem" is the person and "Islam" is the religion. It is good to get clarity about that.

Sacrificial Offerings
Inside the mosque, the threshing rock is located directly under the dome. We can see a hole in the rock where the blood of Jewish sacrifices was drained off into a cave below and then into the brook Hedron. At Passover, 25,000 sheep could be slaughtered. Now we re taking stairs which lead down from the threshing rock into the cave below, and we clearly see traces of blood stains. Now we are leaving the mosque and walking to the Wailing Wall also known as the Western Wall. The Jews, with men and women divided, still give lamentations at the wall. It looks just like pictures I have seen. As I stand near the wall, the past and present melt into a single moment.

Saturday, October 19, 1974 – Jerusalem and Surrounding Area
Via Dolorosa
Saturday is the day we walk the "way of the Cross", known s the Via Dolorosa. We arrive at our starting place in old Jerusalem where we are joined by another tour group. We walk past various "stations" of the cross; each station denotes a memorable event believed to have happened as Jesus carried a massive wood cross on his back while walking to Calvary. The stations along our walk will be where Jesus was sentenced to death, where he is given the cross to carry on his back, where he falls for the first time, where he meets his mother, where Simon helps Jesus carry the cross, where a woman wipes his face, where he falls for the second time, where he talks to the women of Jerusalem, where he falls once more, where he is stripped of his garments, nailed to a cross, and dies. Continued stations are where Jesus is taken down from the cross, where he is laid in the sepulcher, and where he rises from the dead. We have quite a walk ahead of us! What must it have been like for Jesus? It is difficult to imagine such a journey.

We are passing through narrow, dusty, dirty streets. Everywhere there are crowded open shops with wares hanging out for sale; there are trucks delivering items, donkeys carrying goods, souvenir shops, and so many people. The noise of the children is so loud that I barely can hear our guide; at the same time, I must be careful not to slip along winding, rocky, stone alleyways. In the background, I hear seductive Middle East music. I am imagining dancing, laughing, shouting, and the noise of children during the time when Jesus lived. I am remembering how Jesus loved children and said, "Allow the little children to come to me; forbid them not, for such is the kingdom of heaven." Now we are at the end of the city where a city gate was located at the time of Jesus. Here Jesus fell under the heavy cross for the second time; here he said to people surrounding him, "Weep not for me, but for yourselves."

Market activity is everywhere. I am surrounded by fruit and vegetable stands and pottery shops. A woman is standing next to me in a long dress with a basket on her head. Men are pushing carts filled with their wares. New we are passing huge meat hooks with fresh meat carcasses hanging from them. I am thinking the city has changed little since Jesus walked to Calvary. Finally, we arrive at the Church of the Holy Sepulcher where the traditional site of Calvary is located. This is the site recognized by King Constantine. However, we visit a garden tomb, which was excavated in the late 1800s and would seem to be a likely spot. It all ends so suddenly.

Sunday, October 20, 1974 – Leaving Jerusalem
Palestinian Dispersion and The Long Road Back to Amman

It is Sunday, and we are at the airport in Amman, Jordan on the plane waiting for take off. The time is 8:30 p.m., and I am exhausted. We started at eight o'clock this morning from our hotel in Jerusalem. As we crossed the border in our bus, I couldn't believe the sights around us. Taxis and buses were backed up for miles on dusty roads. They were loaded with hot, weary people weighted down with boxes, luggage, paper bags, and anything imaginable that would carry goods. They were returning from the Moslem holiday celebration in Jerusalem. I am told they were checked at nine different checkpoints; at one checkpoint, they must remove all their clothes. They looked so weary and reminded me of one great blob of suffering humanity, stripped of any dignity. And yet, they suffer the consequences to visit Jerusalem and friends and family. They long to be in a place that is sacred to them. As we crossed the border, I was glad to leave Jerusalem and its problems behind me, at least for now. However, I knew that Jerusalem's problems were becoming the world's problems.

As I think back now to Jerusalem, the most prominent thing I remember is the sky at night. It was so clear, and the stars were so brilliant. I can understand why this is the land of the prophets. I think their wisdom must have come, in part, from the clarity of the nights when heaven and earth seem to touch.

The Letter

Here my letter to family and friends ended just as my Middle East experience began; it was a kind of new birth as my life-direction turned away from western civilization to the Middle East. In many ways, it was where I had been heading all my life. The letter was a last desperate attempt to draw Stateside family and friends into my Middle East fate; but this was as far as they could come with me on the journey. My soon to come journey into Riyadh would disconnect me, at least for a time, with my Stateside past. I was afraid of going to Riyadh for fear that I would lose my Christian western self. My letter to Stateside friends and family was my last attempt to hold to my past. Little did I know that Riyadh would open a whole new future for me of university study, political legislative work, and more international travel. My myopic vision was to be expanded beyond imagination as I developed a greater universal understanding.

Cairo, Egypt

In Cairo, we managed enough energy to visit marvelous museums with ancient mummies excavated from king's tombs. Preserved human remains now were under glass, along with too many artifacts to describe. Near the museums, we descended into pyramid tombs accompanied only by our joking guide with a flashlight. I do remember our guide telling us that the pyramids could not be built today because no Cairo bridge could bear the weight of even one stone. Each stone, weighing many tons and carved from distant mountains, was brought to this location and fitted perfectly into each pyramid. After walking, climbing and descending stairways, we were happy to be out of the dark rooms of the dead and the winding corridors of ancient pyramids. Outside, someone spotted an Egyptian man with several camels; so, after paying a fee, we mounted up on camels and laughed at one another while taking photos! It was a happy ending to a memorable trip. In retrospect, the trip – from Beirut to Amman to Petra to the Jordan River to Bethlehem, Jerusalem and surrounding regions, and on to Cairo – was a special gift. All that I saw and experienced would help me in years to come when my life would collide with ancient traditions, religions and beliefs, and with modern geopolitics. My trip instilled in me a greater desire to understand, not only ancient history, but also modern international politics.

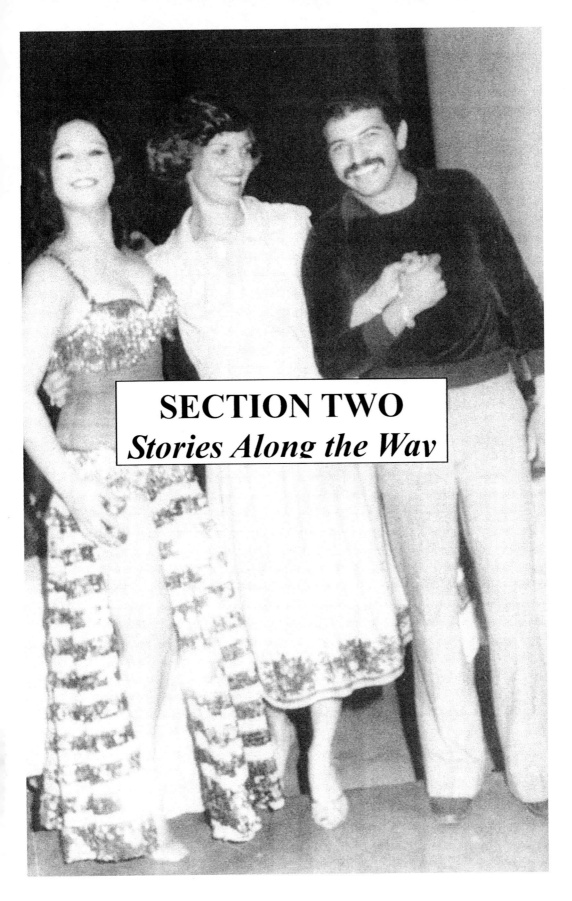

SECTION TWO
Stories Along the Way

UNVEILINGS
A Desert Journey
by
Patricia Adora Clark Taylor

CHAPTER ONE -- MY LIFE IN RIYADH
Riyadh, Saudi Arabia -- 1976

1976 Riyadh – Camels Crossing the Road

August of 1976 found our family standing in the airport in Riyadh, Saudi Arabia. The time was 2 a.m.; the terminal we entered was packed with passengers who arrived with us on the jumbo jet flight from Rome. The small visa and passport check area, which also was the luggage area, was not large enough for the passengers emerging from the large passenger jet. Finally, we got through long lines of people waiting to have visas and passports checked by Saudi guards. Next we stood among crowds of passengers trying to locate luggage. People were pushing and shoving; tired children were crying. Luggage was strewn all around the bare floor. Preston and Allen were guarding our luggage as Chet and I located it. Chet signaled from across the room that he had located another suitcase. As if there was not enough confusion, Julie, our funny looking black dog (part black poodle and part black lab) we acquired in Italy, escaped from her cage with Preston's help. Julie jumped on Preston and Allen with her tail wagging and tried to lick their skin off! She was so happy to see them. Suddenly, a Saudi official witnessing the scene came running over and gestured for them to put Julie back in the cage. It was obvious that he disliked dogs -- and I immediately disliked him and every other Saudi in the world. I had heard that Saudis considered dogs to be unclean and that they were capable of torturing a dog to death for fun. Oh my God, I was in a land of barbarians!

Finally, our entire luggage was together, and we lined up for a customs check hoping to get through quickly because the list of contraband items goes on endlessly. An innocent advertisement with a girl in a bathing suit might be "pornography", and heaven forbid that anything in your possession was made by a "Jewish" company such as my previous employer, Revlon Cosmetics, for whom I worked in Okinawa and in Europe. The Saudi who went through our luggage did not find forbidden items. Then he plunged his hand into my personal bag containing my Bible and other items. I feared they would be tossed away, but I forgot that I placed a sewing needle and thread in my handbag. Suddenly the end of his finger made direct contact with my sewing needle; his finger then went rapidly to his mouth so he could suck the bleeding wound. Disgustedly, he waved us through the luggage area. A guardian angel was protecting us!

A glass see-through partition separated us from a packed waiting room of westerners and Saudis. People strained to get to the partition to see if new employees were among the passengers from Rome. Saudis came for entertainment and amusement. They pointed at us and smiled and laughed as they pressed their faces to the glass to get a close look. Here, a live stage performance was played out each night as people arrived in Riyadh from around the world. To Saudis, the arriving flustered passengers were a sight to behold. They especially enjoyed looking at women who were so brazen as to walk around with faces uncovered! Interspersed throughout the waiting crowd, American looking men, holding company signs such as Lockheed, desperately were trying to find employees. The company names throughout the airport waiting area were European, American, Canadian, and Korean.

A Saudi porter piled our belongings on a cart and began pushing through the crowd. We strained our necks to see familiar faces. Suddenly Patti and Joe Arcari with their two daughters, Anela and Sarena who were the ages of Preston and Allen, broke through the crowd and came running toward us. We all hugged; then Patti and Joe were laughing and saying, "Don't do it! Go back! Go back! You don't know what you are getting into here in Riyadh! Then we saw two other good friends, Dirk and JoAnn Decker, coming to meet us. We were happy to see more friendly faces; and they whisked us off, including Julie, into the black night to our temporary living quarters where we arrived at 4 a.m., unpacked a few items, and fell into bed. Julie was serenely curled up on the floor.

I awoke about 11 a.m. to the sound of the window air conditioner with its constant whirring sound. It never cut back, just roared on and on in the hot, dry August weather. I knew the temperature would reach 120 degrees. The dry, stale smell of the desert already was in my nostrils. The curtains at the window refused to keep back the sun. Slowly I tried to orientate myself to my surroundings. Where was I? I noticed that the floor was cluttered with scattered suitcases, some quickly opened to get us through the night. The unorganized sight brought back the memory of airplanes and airports. Preston and Allen were still sleeping in the other bedroom of our small apartment. We were in temporary living quarters until our large concrete block desert house, complete with nine foot high concrete walls all around, was ready for us. Chet was up early and at work. That was no surprise. Chet rarely missed a day of work. Today it would be necessary for him to get his assigned car so we could get out and get necessary photos and identification badges. We also needed groceries from the small commissary for our kitchen here in our apartment. As I walked into the living room, I saw a note slipped under the door. I opened it and was happy to see that it was from Patti. The note read, "Welcome! Come up to our apartment for coffee and breakfast. Bring the boys!" I had prayed that God would go ahead of us in this barren land and prepare the way. He sent Patti as an answer to prayer.

Allen and Preston awoke and dressed; Chet arrived home from work for lunch. Joe also arrived, and we converged on Patti at the same time. It was like a family reunion! We sat around eating the delicious food prepared by Patti. We were talking, asking questions, and answering questions all at once. Patti and Joe are people with a great attitude. Life for them is an adventure. Patti is one of the most industrious persons I ever met. She is the only person I know who can pack to go to Europe while making Christmas cookies, planning a dinner party, baking a cake for someone's birthday and always remembering to attend Catholic mass.

After lunch, we were in for a surprise; Chet took us for our first trip around Riyadh! We found it to be such a strange place. Everywhere we looked we saw white Toyota pickup trucks with many different colorful designs and all kinds of colorful paraphernalia hanging inside and outside. Many trucks hauled goats crowded into the back with an entire family in the small cab in the front. Sometimes men and boys sat up front and women and girls sat in back with the goats or whatever cargo was being hauled. Sometimes we would see a camel kneeling in the back of the pickup truck. It was such a sight to see the camel with its long neck and huge head sticking out of the back of the little truck. Times definitely were changing; even camels rode in trucks! We drove towards the middle of the downtown shopping area. We headed down King Faisal Street where wood framed shops with glass windows showed off glistening gold jewelry. This was one of the gold suqs (marketplaces) in Riyadh. Everywhere I looked, opulence was encased by crudeness. Even the more modern buildings looked crude by western standards. Paper and debris of all sorts cluttered streets and sidewalks. Many streets were not paved, giving a kind of "western movie look" in areas. How I missed seeing the great cathedrals and museums of Florence where I had walked freely along cobblestone streets.

We turned off King Faisal Street and entered old market places within the city area where I would learn to find everything from cooking utensils to brassware. Further down the street was a market that sold wonderful fruits and vegetables. Some of the most beautiful melons I have ever seen could be found here. Close by was the old women's suq which was an open air market displaying woven baskets and handmade silver jewelry. The women, dressed from head to toe with swirling yards of black fabric clothing, sat cross-legged on the dusty ground beckoning me to come and look, come and buy beautiful items. As I examined their wares, I noticed animal bones scattered around the area on the dirt streets. I saw what I thought were goat hoofs, tails, and various other bones. It occurred to me that this location was also for animal slaughtering.

Here in the very heart of the city was a heart stopping scene. In the midst of the oppressive heat and the dust, there were so many black-veiled women! The "veil" was not just a flimsy little veil that covered the face just below the eyes as is often depicted in movies. The veil was a hideous square shaped black piece of thick gauze material that covered the woman like a tent from the top of her head to her feet and imprisoned her for life. Under this black gauze material was a face mask which was a separate piece of black material with two slits cut out for the eyes and strings on the side to be tied behind the head. Under the gauze tent known as the "obiya" was a long black dress which covered the ankles and the arms. The women went under this black covering at puberty and stayed covered for the rest of their lives. A woman was allowed to unveil only at home with the harem of other women or in the presence of a husband or father. Saudi women were rarely with men. Their homes had separate entrances. One entrance was for men and one was for women. (It was rumored that when Queen Elizabeth of England visited Saudi Arabia, she entered the palace through a woman's entrance.) From the time of their youth, males and females live separate lives. There seems to be no real affection between husband and wife. The Koran (the holy book of Islam) allows men to have five wives and to easily divorce any wife by saying several times, "I divorce you." Automatically, the man gets any children. Women are left to friends and family for any care. The best opportunity for Saudi women, with no chance for education, is to be born into a wealthy family. Later, while living in Saudi, I met an American woman who was married for fifteen years to a Saudi man. They met and married while attending a university in California. She accompanied him back to his home in Saudi, and they had several children. He later divorced her and married another woman. I asked her what her personal life was like while married to this man. She answered that there was no real relationship. Her husband came to her from time to time for sex and then left her. She lived exclusively with the harem, meaning the other women in the family including her mother-in-law, her husband's sisters, and other women relatives. After they divorced, she returned to the States and lectured about her Saudi experience. From time to time, because of sympathetic Saudi friends, she was allowed back in the country to see her children.

We turned away from the women's suq and walked down another side street; suddenly we were at the infamous "Headchoppers Square." Several streets converge at this spot, and the largest mosque in Riyadh was located just across from the square. On the other side of the square was a government building known as the Mayor's Building. In the center of the square was the Clock Tower -- a tall obelisk with a clock at the top. The base of this tower provided the spot where human heads and hands were cut off for punishment and women were stoned to death for adultery.

A block away was the Abd al Aziz Fort, an old clay structure. This was the historic location where a youthful Abd al Aziz, in the early part of the 20th century, made a surprise attack and killed the pro-Ottoman family of Rashidi. During the next ten years, he conquered other provinces from the Rashidi family. On September 18, 1932, by royal decree, the dual kingdom of Nazd and Hejaz became the "Kingdom of Saudi Arabia."

We drove to another part of Riyadh to the old guest palace of Abd al Aziz where ranking Bedouin had been welcome as guests of the king. Joyful occasions such as weddings took place here. Across the road was a large water tower with a restaurant on top. The restaurant was available only for private events, partly for security reasons because it overlooked government office buildings including the King's Office, where King Faisal was assassinated by a relative in the early 1970s. Nearby the King's Office or the Royal Office was the Office of Ministries which formally was a palace of King Saud who was king before Faisal. This structure also was known as the Red Palace because of its noticeable red color. Most of Riyadh was dismal, dusty, and brown; however the government was making an effort to beautify some of the city by planting date palms and blooming bushes along main streets; and I spotted a few green grassy areas. Also, palaces were surrounded by lush green lawns, flowering bushes, and tall date palms. All that was required to make the desert bloom with vivid, vibrant color was water. Saudi Arabia, blessed with oil, had little water.

1976 Riyadh – King Faisal's Office Building

We continued on to Sumaysi Street with its large Central Hospital with free care for the people and the nearby newly constructed Museum of Antiquities which highlighted historic items from recent excavations throughout Saudi Arabia. Next we left Riyadh and drove eastward toward the palaces of former King Faisal, now belonging to current King Khaled and the heir to the throne, Prince Fahd. Finally we were seeing some greenery. The sky was a clear blue, the sun was bright; outside our air-conditioned automobile, the temperature was climbing. The paved black highway stretched out across the beige desert for as far as we could see and sent up a steamy mirage. Through the waves of heat emerging from the blistering hot road, we occasionally could see a truck, car, or bus on the distant horizon. There was an almost eerie feeling of traveling across the moon.

I began to take notice of automobiles traveling along the two lane highway. Around town and even here on the desert highway, I saw mostly Toyota pickup trucks and Mercedes sedans. I also spotted General Motors cars; we were assigned a wine colored Pontiac four door sedan with wine plush interior. I assumed us Corps of Engineers folks in Saudi got the odd colored autos that were difficult to sell in the states. The color made little difference to me; I was thankful for air-conditioning! No Ford products could be seen anywhere; they were not allowed into Saudi Arabia because Ford had a manufacturing plant in Israel. The products of any American company were banned if the company had a manufacturing plant in Israel.

As we passed the palace of King Khaled, I saw a Rolls Royce enter the gates. During my stay in Riyadh, I realized that Rolls Royce is "the car" of the Saudi Royal Family. Many are seen throughout Riyadh. Another common sight was that of street lights knocked down in a twisted form on the ground by the side of the road. The city was full of damaged light poles. I learned the reason. It is not unusual for a Saudi man (women are not allowed to drive) to buy a new automobile and ask the salesman where to put the key and how one's feet work on the pedals. With a bit of information, they drive away. Soon afterwards the car may be wrecked. Light poles seem to be the bulwark for stopping runaway cars from further damage. In such an accident, the Saudi leaves the car and walks away. If he wants another one, he will buy another one. Money is not the issue. The Saudi government tries to keep wrecked cars off the streets, but accidents happen so rapidly that there are always plenty of wrecked cars and wrecked light poles to be seen. Light poles are changed regularly, but trying to keep up with the demand seems an impossible task. Chet had to be a defensive driver because of inept Saudi drivers, some with eye diseases because of all the flies which suck moisture from the eyes. Other drivers have no peripheral vision because of their headdress or "gutra" which hangs loosely around their head and results in a kind of tunnel vision for the wearer.

From the palace, we headed further east, turned off the highway, and drove onto the rocky brown desert. On our left we saw the horizon of Riyadh. Just ahead of us, we could see the beginning of a sports complex, which was to be a new city providing climate controlled structures for sports events and spectators. Hotels, motels, and a hospital would be included in the construction plan. As we drove past the desert site, Chet told me about the 13,000 acre sports city, large enough, the Saudis figured, for a future Summer Olympics. Twenty minutes away by car was another large construction site, the new University of Riyadh. That day, only desert could be seen with building cranes scattered throughout the site; but the plans were drawn and during our three years in Saudi, we saw the university emerge from the desert. Incidentally, the building crane was jokingly known as the national bird of Saudi Arabia because cranes could be seen everywhere! The construction build-up of Saudi Arabia was in full swing! As part of the build-up, the modern university would be completed in a few years with twelve million square feet of buildings and a huge mosque at the university center with walkways extending outwards from the mosque to all other buildings. The teachings of Islam would be the foundation for any learning at this university.

Later, as I remembered that day, I wondered where the people would come from to utilize these facilities. Certainly, it was all too much for the migrant, unlearned Saudi; and half of the population, Saudi women, was not allowed to attend school. But within the three years that I was in Saudi, I witnessed the Saudi Moslem plan taking shape. People for these facilities would come from all over the world as Saudi Arabia became, with all its riches, a Moslem showplace for the world. Poor people, rich people, skilled, unskilled would be brought here and given lodging and education -- and always with Islam as the center of teaching and the foundation for education.

Further along in the desert, we went down, down, down into a river bed known as a "wadi." These snake-like wadis spread across Saudi Arabia like so many fingers. In the lush green wadi areas there are miles and miles of farmland. Fruits, vegetables, and countless date trees with huge delicious dates are grown for private use and for marketing. As we wound down through the river bed known as Wadi Hanifa, we saw crude farms with flat roofed clay structures among tall date palms. Children, sheep, and goats all frolicked together. It was a scene from the Old Testament. The slender barefoot children were beautiful with their black hair and dark round eyes. Little girls with long black wavy hair and long print cotton dresses ran barefoot in the dirt. The children laughed and shouted and waved to us.

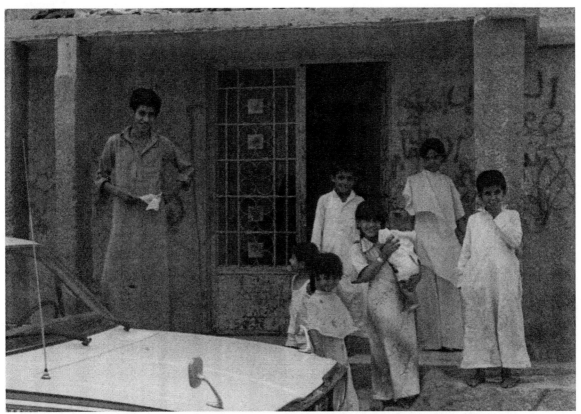

1976 Saudi Children – Wadi Hanifa near Riyadh

A wadi was an interesting source of life. I learned that these river beds flood every several years. During dry years, plant seeds and tiny animal life remained dormant, then suddenly would spring to life in the rain, only to sleep once more for a season. But when it rained, oh what a beautiful sight! During my three years in Saudi Arabia, I remember seeing this only once. My memory is of flowing water, green riverbanks, and colorful flowers.

UNVEILINGS
A Desert Journey
by
Patricia Adora Clark Taylor

CHAPTER TWO -- MY DESERT HOME
Riyadh, Saudi Arabia -- 1976

Our family visits the Riyadh Camel Races and encounters the Saudi National Guard

After several weeks, Patti and I, together with our families, moved into our new living quarters. Words seem inadequate to describe our desert life. First of all, we were located in the middle of the desert. There were no roads leading to our villas. There was only hard, bumpy, rocky, barren, desert. There was no greenery within miles. Debris of all sorts cluttered the otherwise barren land. Houses were under construction in our general area, but none were completed. The only nearby completed structure was a mosque located directly across from our compound that blared the Moslem call to prayer five times daily -- right into our homes. A nine foot concrete wall surrounded our four family compound, separating us from the outside world. The wall had gates that locked. Within our wall, all was brown and barren. Our houses were painted white to deflect some of the blaring hot sun. Our compound consisted of two large two-story structures built in a back to back design. Each had a flat roof with a wall around the roof. We could not see out our windows, but on the roof we could look out over the desert. The roof had a water tank to store water delivered on a regular basis by a huge Mercedes water truck. A pump for each living quarters pumped the water up to rooftop water tanks. Each of the cement block housing structures housed two families in townhouse fashion. Patti and I chose quarters in the same structure. We had not yet met the other two families who would complete our four-family compound. Patti and I prayed that they would be friendly and easy to get along with because we all would be living together!

Patti's cheerfulness was contagious and soon we were moved in and making our quarters livable. Each of our houses was large with high ceilings and with chandeliers in the living areas. Upstairs bedrooms were huge; I once remarked that Preston could play basketball in his bedroom. The flooring throughout was a hard white concrete terrazzo The large kitchen was fully furnished with the latest appliances. The furniture throughout the house was large and comfortable, colorful carpets covered some of the hard floor. Our draperies were the last housing item to be delivered; when they came, we were ready to party!

When Joe and Chet left us in the morning, Patti and I had no way to communicate with them. We had no contact with the outside world. We had no phone, radio, nothing. It was a strange feeling to be locked behind a nine foot concrete wall. I found myself wondering, "Why here, Lord?" In the solitude of this barren land, I turned my face more and more to the God of the universe; His presence became my strength.

1976 -- Riyadh Neighborhood Under Construction

My heart went out to Preston. If only I could have seen then how God was going to bless him through the years in Saudi. But all I could see was an unhappy eight year old boy with his adoring black dog Julie; both were locked behind a nine foot wall. Julie had roamed freely, racing behind Preston on his bike in our Italian town of Tirrenia. Oh, how I missed Italy! Allen had returned to school at the end of the summer; he was happy to be returning to school in Florida! Preston stayed behind and entered the Riyadh International School where he met children from countries such as England, Germany, Italy, Switzerland, Japan, Korea, and Canada. For most of these children, school was an outlet from houses like ours behind barren walls. School was a place for children to make friends. Often Preston came home with an invitation to a birthday party. The note would contain a crude map with landmarks such as a big hole in the road, a Pepsi Cola shack, You and Your Kid Dress Shop, building under construction, the water tower, the pink mosque, the black marble palace, Intercontinental Hotel, Headchopper's Square, the gold suq, the vegetable suq, King Khaled's palace, Prince Fahd's palace, and a long list of familiar and not so familiar landmarks.

Occasionally, a landmark would disappear. One Corps of Engineers family had Bedouin neighbors with large tents and goat pens living across the road. It was an easy to recognize landmark until one day, without warning, the Bedouin moved on!

Preston's birthday party with school friends

Change was everywhere. Riyadh would never be the same. One day a roadway would be completely dug up in order to put down telephone lines. Later, it would become a road again, only to be dug up again for drainage pipes. At any time, getting around was confusing because of all the construction. One friend who remembered the rebuilding of Germany after World War II, said Riyadh looked about the same. Rubble and potholes were everywhere, making driving even more hazardous. A detour could be disastrous, particularly at night in the unlit desert. A car easily could run into a big hole left carelessly with no signs around. So when Preston was invited to a birthday party, it always was a feat to get him there and back home.

I, too, was getting out more and making new friends. Chet rarely could drive me since most of my activities were during the day. Therefore, I relied on Army Corps of Engineer drivers assigned to women. We were pleased and privileged to have drivers, but there were always problems. Drivers could be late or not show at all. Many of the drivers were Yemen from a country south of Saudi Arabia and were just learning their way around Riyadh, but they were polite even when they were lost. The Corps drivers had a good sense of humor and were trusted to get us from place to place. Humorous driving stories abounded, and when we were together with others, story telling was great entertainment and an outlet for day to day frustrations! Most families entertained regularly. Dinner parties became a source of great fun and camaraderie developed among Corps families and with many others, also.

In September after Patti and I moved into our villas, a third American family, the Jones family, arrived at our compound. There was Cecil who was a lieutenant colonel and supply officer, his wife Randy who was a nurse, and their son Timmy who was a cute two year old! One night I spotted them through my living room window which looked directly into their living room window. Chet and I went over to meet them. Randy was glaring at Cecil and demanding to know what he had gotten her into by bringing her to such a god-forsaken place! By now I understood culture shock; Randy had it. She also was exhausted because of the long trip from New York to London to Riyadh. Over the next few days, Patti and I discovered that Randy had a great sense of humor. As both a nurse and a humorist, Randy was the perfect asset for our compound! Randy brought a medical kit from the States that became handy on various occasions. Soon after arriving, Randy became the school nurse at Riyadh International School and was a blessing to many children who had no other medical care. Randy knew how to heal hurt feelings, and she was a good listener for children who struggled with their own difficulties.

Finally, in October, as we prayed for just the right family to complete our compound, the McBrayers arrived from North Carolina! Homer McBrayer, a civil engineer like Chet, employed by the Corps of Engineers, was tall and lanky with a kind face. His tall, attractive wife Jackie had short blond hair and a great smile. Their two sons, Chip and Brad, were about Preston's age. Hurray for Preston! A mighty Chihuahua named Bruce completed the family. Hurray for Julie!

After their arrival, I knocked on Jackie's door to introduce myself. I wondered what she would be like as I waited for her to come to the door. After awhile, she peeked out of a small window beside the door; only then did she open the door. She had been crying, and she apologized for her frantic state of mind. Jackie had a severe case of culture shock! She almost was too frightened to open the door, even for me. My heart went out to her. She cried continuously the first few weeks she was in Saudi. I honestly thought Jackie would not adapt, and that she would return to the States. How wrong I was about her! Over time, Jackie, who was a wonderful hostess, blossomed in Riyadh like no one else. People throughout Saudi Arabia came to the McBrayer home and experienced their warm and generous hospitality. Jackie could be a friend like no other; one who would laugh and cry with others. Jackie, an efficient, well-organized administrator, soon began working for a company in Riyadh. That left Pattie and me alone in the compound during the day. Randy hired a sitter for Timmie, the other children were in school during the day. Chet and the other men sometimes worked long hours. Our weekends were Thursday and Friday, rather than Saturday and Sunday, because Friday is the Moslem holy day. Even when Chet was gone, I had no trouble getting around by going places with other wives and their husbands or with drivers.

My first year in Riyadh, Patti and I spent a lot of time together. Rarely was there a dull moment! One of our first ventures was a luncheon at our compound for seventy women. Not just an ordinary luncheon; we decided to have a luau! Both Patti and I had lived in Hawaii, and we decided to make the luau as authentic as possible considering the circumstances. There would be no roasted pig because pigs were considered by Saudis to be "unclean." But we decided on a Polynesian menu, and then went to work making colorful tissue paper flowers. Before long, we enlisted other wives to make colorful decorations that would transform our houses with a South Sea atmosphere. My house would be the first luncheon stop where fruit punch and exotic hordevours ("pupus" in Hawaiian) would be served to our guests. We removed the furniture from Patti's living room and dining room and enlisted men to borrow wood doors from a nearby construction site. The doors were placed lengthwise on the floors with pillows from our furniture placed underneath the doors at the ends to elevate each door several inches, transforming them into long, low tables. We removed all the furniture pillows from all four houses and covered Patti's floors with "tables" and pillows. The men went to a nearby riverbed area and cut long palm fronds from date palms. We covered the tables and the walls with palm fronds and then used tissue paper flowers everywhere. Patti's house became a house of greenery and colorful flowers with long tables lined up and soft pillows to sit on. The day before the luncheon, Patti and I began cooking early in the morning and cooked all day. The pork purchased from the US commissary became sweet and sour pork. In addition, we had chicken soya, and beef with vegetables. Patti and I both had large rice cookers, and we cooked lots of rice the next morning. Our meat dishes were stored overnight in big freezers in our houses. Early the next morning we turned our ovens on and began heating food. By noon, we were ready for seventy guests! When the guests arrived, they were invited into my house for punch and pupus. The women had no idea what awaited them in Patti's house. After a time of getting acquainted, our guests were escorted into Patti's house. All these women, fighting a hostile desert environment each day, were suddenly standing in the midst of a tropical paradise! Soft, lovely Hawaiian music was playing in a cool green environment with flowers everywhere. The tables were beautifully set, and our guests were served delicious food. They were amazed at the transformation! Patti and I and others who helped us were excited; we actually changed our environment momentarily into something friendly, colorful, and beautiful! I always will remember that exciting day; and to this very day, I believe women still talk about that luau!

**SARINA AT LEFT; PATTI AT RIGHT
CENTER IS A DEDICATED LUAU HELPER**

As I think back to that time in my life, I realize how much God blessed that little compound in the middle of the desert. A rare friendship was forged between Patti and me. I came to love Patti and her daughters Anela and Sarina who were as talented and lovely as Patti. Joe also was delightful, easygoing, and thoughtful. Joe was an intellectual and, more than other men, sympathized with women in Saudi Arabia. He was the one who, almost always, could be counted on to help. Later, when they relocated to Germany, we remained friends.

UNVEILINGS
A Desert Journey
by
Patricia Adora Clark Taylor

CHAPTER THREE -- MY DESERT CHURCH
Riyadh, Saudi Arabia -- 1976

1976 -- Riyadh Ruins – Saudi Man with Goats

Dr. Dudley Woodberry and his wife Roberta, who were missionaries with the Presbyterian Mission Board in Kabul, Afghanistan, arrived in Riyadh with their three handsome sons about the same time of our arrival. Western companies in Riyadh were seeking a Christian minister. The ruling royal family verbally concurred, which was no small miracle. Christianity is unlawful in Saudi Arabia and is not tolerated; Moslem dissenters face death as punishment.

While in Kabul, the Woodberrys heard about the search for a minister; they decided to come to Riyadh knowing that there was some risk surrounding such a position. First of all, they had to dissociate themselves with any mission board, thereby forfeiting both financial and spiritual benefits. Further, they would be at the mercy of Christians in Riyadh for their salary, housing, schooling for children, automobiles, companionship, etc. However, they knew that Riyadh was where God was leading them. One of the U.S. companies arranged for visas. Dudley would be listed as a "welfare counselor", a title not endearing to him or Roberta. Nevertheless, shortly after we arrived in Riyadh, our "welfare counselor" and family arrived in this desert land.

Dudley and Roberta, both U.S. citizens, met in the 1950s in Lebanon when Roberta was studying at a girl's school in Beirut. Dudley, born to missionary parents in China, was working on his doctorate in Islamic studies. Roberta, the daughter of a minister in the States, had a beautiful soprano voice; music was her passion. I still remember her singing in our Riyadh gatherings, "His eye is on the sparrow and I know He watches me." She shared Dudley's love and concern for the Middle East and his appreciation for the history and culture of Islamic people.

Protestant Christians in Riyadh were meeting on one of the U.S. military bases in the recreation center auditorium. Dudley and Roberta would be in charge of these services. Catholic Christians met on another U.S. military base in another recreation center. The centers were closed off from the road by high walls. Protestant services and Catholic masses were swelling in number as people from different parts of the world, working together in Saudi, attended the meetings. Saudis were absolutely forbidden; also, cars of persons attending services were parked inconspicuously on side streets, so that no notice of a crowd could be taken by any Saudi.

In spite of caution about services, we were happy to meet together to worship and fellowship. Without a doubt, God was with us. When I think back on those services, I remember only the wonderful people because there was no church building. Our family attended the eleven a.m. service and often waited outside for Arab Christian services to end. Even thought Saudis could not be Christians, there were many Arab Christians from surrounding countries. Our wait provided a chance to visit with friends such as Mary Brooks and Sandro. Mary Brooks, with Sandro at her side, would be smiling a big lovely smile and waving to us. We all would embrace and share the past week's events. Mary Brooks was blond, stately, slender, and attractive. Born in North Carolina, she had been a newspaper reporter and later studied seriously for the theater. During her acting years, she visited northern Italy and met a handsome and intelligent engineer, Sandro Zucherelli. They fell in love, had a short engagement, and married. After a time, they moved to Riyadh where Sandro represented an Italian construction company and managed work throughout Saudi Arabia. Our friendship was forged from the first time we met together; we really hit it off! Others in the congregation were from England, Germany, Holland, Pakistan, Egypt, Lebanon, Canada, Australia, Korea, Thailand, Philippines, and many other countries. It was exciting to see faces from around the world.

I remember celebrating the Lord's Supper with a Pakistani woman, dressed in the traditional sari, seated next to me. She had three small children with her; one was a baby in her arms. When the bread was passed, she pinched off a small piece for each child and placed it in their mouth while repeating the words, "This is because Jesus loves you." I was touched by that scene. To this day, sharing the Lord's Supper reminds me of that woman and her children. In Saudi, the Lord's Supper was more meaningful, in part, because we were a truer picture of the Body of Christ. Also, the presence of God was real. To this day, I have never experienced a church service in the U.S. that gave me such a sense of community with people of the world. Sometimes American style Christianity is like "sounding brass," giving out a hollow sound that chills to the bone. It is fraught with its own prejudice, its own selfishness, and its overwhelming desire to build mega-churches and acquire mega-wealth at the expense of dedicated love and service to widows, orphans, the poor, and people in need. No where did Jesus say, "Build mega-churches and get rich. Admire wealthy religious leaders. As for those in need, forget them; they are an embarrassment."

Dr. Woodberry taught me about the importance of eating together. In Middle East countries, to sit and eat together denotes a special relationship. Eating is a personal activity of great enjoyment, and food preparation is the key to an excellent meal. An important part of Middle East hospitality is inviting guests to partake of a meal. At the table, a great deal of exclaiming is done about the taste and the preparation of the food. The table is set with a variety of foods such as round Arabic bread, egg dishes, meat and vegetable dishes, and rice dishes. Fruit is served for desert, sometimes with a pastry coated with honey and pine nuts. A wife takes pride in selecting the freshest ingredients and mixing them with fragrant spices. The food must be a feast for the eye with just the right mix of textures and colors. The meal is a celebration and provides the perfect opportunity for fellowship. Under the leadership of Dr. Woodberry, I understood more about the privilege of being part of the Lord's Supper.

During my three years in Saudi, Dr. Woodberry taught us about the patriarchs of the Bible and about the world in which they lived, taught, and wrote scriptures which survive into modern times. Daily in the desert, I saw long-ago scenes unfold before my eyes. The Bedouin, the true Saudis, are the children of Ishmael and his father Abraham. Bedouin tribal law is bases literally upon Old Testament law which requires, "an eye for an eye and a tooth for a tooth." Since ancient times, the Bedouin travel the desert in tribal fashion taking their belongings with them. To this day, Bedouin lifestyle relies upon the camel which provides them with milk and desert transportation. Camels are of great value, and although Bedouin will eat camel, rarely is a camel killed. The desert today continues to be dotted with long, low, dark-colored Bedouin tents with herds of goat and camel nearby. Sometimes, even inside the city, an old man with a long white beard is seen herding his sheep or goats along streets and through market places while completely oblivious to the traffic and confusion of the city.

One weekend, Chet, Preston, and I, along with the Arcari family, drove outside the city and down into the wadi where we drove along the dry river bottom and saw many date farms. Once we stopped and walked among the date trees, enjoying their rich green color and the shade provided by the trees. Suddenly, a shepherdess came toward us with sheep. She was veiled in black, but her face was uncovered; she took little notice of us. Old looking and weather worn, her skin showed the price extracted from the harshness of the climate. In retrospect, I realize that Bedouin seem to take little notice of the modern civilization forced upon their ancient lifestyle. Probably, the old ones will live out their lives much as their ancestors have for thousands of years, but the young will never be able to return to the past. Time caught up with the Middle East; and just as the Saudi cannot return to life as it was, neither can any of us ever return to previous times. World events have changed the way we all live. In the 1930s, oil was pumped from Saudi Arabia; in the 1040s, Israel became a nation. These two facts brought us to a crossroads in history, playing out a dangerous game of global politics and global economics.

The three years that I lived in Saudi, I considered the miracle of Ishmael and his children. They are a miracle because Hagar, Ishmael's mother, would have died in the desert with her son if God had not intervened and spoken directly to her. He heard her cry for help; God told her to call her son Ishmael which means, "whom God hears." God named Ishmael and blessed him. The story is in the Bible in Genesis, chapters 16 and 17. The Jews, the early record keepers, realized the miracle and recorded the story. Whatever differences there are between the children of Isaac and the children of Ishmael, there is no doubt that both are sons of Abraham. According to ancient Bible stories, God allowed each of them to be born; later God saved each of them from imminent death; and finally, God blessed them.

1976 – Riyadh Tent with Camel Saddle

After the time of father Abraham, the children of Israel and the children of Ishmael went in different directions. The children of Ishmael (whose mother Hagar was an Egyptian) stayed within the nomadic desert culture or settled in areas along major trade rotes. The children of Israel went into captivity into Egypt and became master builders, house servants, and the "worker bees" of Egypt. Later, leaving Egypt, Jews (Hebrews) went through a series of transformations, crossing into Jericho with a "holy book" of early recorded history together with basic laws (the Ten Commandments). However, even earlier, Abraham himself, the father of Israel and Ishmael, must have come out of Ur (modern day Iraq) with a knowledge of law, commerce, farming, and civilization. Without a doubt, both Jews and Arabs have an Egyptian influence together with the influence of Ur, the ancient Sumerian city on the Euphrates River. Jesus himself is connected to the Arab world; the language he spoke was Aramaic which is an Arabic language dialect.

To my knowledge, the world of Islam has no problem with the historic Jesus as a great man and a great prophet. Moslems simply cannot understand or accept that God would allow his own child to be killed on a cross. Interestingly, it is Jesus that seems to be the stumbling block to both Jews and Arabs. When we put Christianity, with its western Roman democratic heritage, into the Arab-Israeli mix, the whole pot of stew gets even more interesting. By the time we get to Jerusalem, with its historic threshing rock which is sacred to Arabs, Jews, and Christians, we are almost at the door of World War III as Jews, Arabs, and Christians fight over land ownership in ancient Palestine or Israel. But does it have to be so? There is common ground. Ultimately, there is a common ancient heritage. At least, it is a starting place.

UNVEILINGS
A Desert Journey
by
Patricia Adora Clark Taylor

CHAPTER FOUR -- TEMPORARY ESCAPE
Riyadh, Saudi Arabia -- 1976

By October 1976, Randy, Patti and I had been behind our wall in Riyadh for almost three months. Europe was the place to go for time out and a change of scenery. Jackie, the last of us to arrive in Riyadh, said she would wait for the next trip. During the end of October, Patti would be in Germany with her daughter Sarina for Sarina's orthodontist visit. There was no orthodontist in Riyadh for Americans, therefore monthly medivac flights to Germany were provided for military personnel and their families who required such medical care. When Patti and Sarina were in Germany in September, they gathered information about the festive annual Christmas Bazaar at the Frankfurt Officers Club. Patti, gregarious as ever, made good friends in Frankfurt on the military base. She learned that vendors throughout Europe come to the bazaar to market special Christmas decorative items and Christmas gift items. During the first week of November, the Officers Club is transformed into a Christmas extravaganza with a breathtaking array of European items. Randy and I managed to get a half price fare on Saudia Airlines to Rome. We decided to fly to Rome and take the train to Frankfurt. I spoke Italian enough to get us around Italy. Randy, who lived in Germany as a child when her father was an officer in the US Army, remembered enough German to get us around Germany. Our husbands, together with friends, would manage the care of our children.

At the end of October, Chet and Cecil took Randy and me to the airport in Riyadh. From Riyadh, we flew to Jeddah, a Saudi city on the Red Sea, to make airline connections to Rome. The small Jeddah airport was crowded as usual and passengers were waving tickets in the air and pushing and shoving their way to the ticket counter. I saw weary eyed people from all parts of the world who were sleeping on whatever possessions they had with them. Their possessions generally were rolled up like a big bed roll. It was the beginning of the Saudi weekend and foreign workers were flying out to various destinations. Flies were everywhere, as they are all over Saudi. Intermingled with destitute looking persons were western businessmen, clutching their briefcases and looking harried and tired. And always there were Koreans who did much of the actual construction labor in Saudi. Usually they were lined up politely around their leader listening carefully for instructions.

I spotted a few families with crying children. All the family members carried their specified items, even the children. And always, there were the black veiled women; it was impossible to get away from them. They were like funny little ghouls who lumbered along or squatted cross-legged up against a wall or in a corner. Rarely was human contact made because of the black facade which shielded them from the world. On occasion, a woman might unveil her face if in a place as cosmopolitan as an airport, and I might see a lovely, smiling face. Sometimes the face would be haughty and angry. Veiled women could be particularly nasty to unveiled women. I never could decide if they resented their veil and their own smothering culture which went with it and envied the freedom of western women, or if they were arrogant and proud of their wealth which some Saudi women displayed with jeweled gold bracelets from the wrist to the elbow. Actually, Saudis, both men and women are a proud people. I believe they were arrogant when they had only sheep and goats and camels. Now they have sports cars and palaces. Nevertheless, regarding Saudi women, I could not see that their status ever changed. They remained imprisoned women, veiled for life, even if they did have gold. Some of the wealthy women could fly away briefly and unveil; but what did it matter? They eventually would return home and veil themselves once more. Apparently, when Mohammed wrote the Koran, he gave no status to women other than to be used by men.

Once we were in our assigned seats, Randy and I waited for the plane to take off. In a moment we would be leaving all of this behind. We were going to Europe and smell the rain and the cool, crisp days! Maybe we would see snow! As the plane left the runway, I felt as if some sinister force might draw us back to the land and the secluded life. But higher and higher we went, and the feeling was exhilarating. We had broken free. We were leaving a black hole; every ounce of force was needed to break free! I was remembering the God we serve who broke the chains for men and women alike. The day Jesus spoke to that "scarlet women" at the well and the day Jesus kept men from stoning a woman to death, he broke the taboos of the human race and ushered women fully into an equal status with men. He let the world know that God's love, grace, and pardon are available for women, as well as men. All of us together, men and women, are the human race. It is not just about men. I know of no other religious tradition that provides such freedom for women.

Randy was seated next to a Saudi businessman who was expounding the virtues of Islam, particularly the part about having five wives. He disapproved of Randy and me having a holiday for ourselves. I told him it might be good for men to have five wives if women could have five husbands. He said that could not be possible. I answered, "Oh yes it is; just look at Elizabeth Taylor." He was quiet for the rest of the trip.

At the end of a five hour flight, the plane touched down at the Rome airport. This time the Rome airport looked lovely and civilized. How could I ever have criticized such a wonderful place? I questioned an Alitalia Airlines employee about flights to Milan. The time was three a.m. She said, if we purchased tickets now, we qualified for a night fare which was half the day fare. We bought our tickets and boarded the small aircraft for Milan. As we deplaned in Milan, I remembered being in this beautiful city two years ago with Chet when we attended LaScala Theater to see the ballet Swan Lake and to watch the great dancer, Rudolph Nureyev. But for now, Randy and I were anxious to get to the Christmas Bazaar in Frankfurt.

We got our luggage, headed for the train station, purchased our train tickets, and waited in the massive, cold lobby with its high-domed ceiling. After a two hour wait, we boarded the train and entered our compartment. I was excited because riding European trains reminds me of scenes from intriguing mystery movies. Soon we were on our way. As we boarded, we learned we were on the scenic tour. It would take us eight hours on this train to get to Frankfurt. It didn't matter about the hours ahead. Nothing could stop our exhilaration! The day unfolded in the crisp morning air. As we rode through Switzerland, there was a smell of morning dew and tall evergreen trees. The train chugged along, up into mountains and down into valleys. We were riding the "local" which stopped at every little village; the scenery was breathtaking! Standing outside our compartment, we held onto the train railing which separated us from the grass and trees beyond, as the air touched our faces. The color green was all about us; the tall evergreen trees seemed to stretch out their long, graceful branches toward us. Sometimes the green forests would wind down and around the mountainside into a clear blue lake reflecting the surrounding scene. I was happy enough to cry!

During those hours, I asked God to help me love the desert and the desert people. I knew God commanded us to love and not sit in judgment of others. Nevertheless, I thought it impossible to love anything about Saudi Arabia; even though I knew God loved the Saudis. Certainly, God was generous in His blessing to them, having given Saudi Arabia blue skies, beautiful sunsets, and immense natural wealth.

When Randy and I arrived in Frankfurt, Patti, who had a comfortable room ready for us, said we were within walking distance of the Frankfurt Officers Club if we wanted to get an early glimpse of the bazaar. Patti, who had been working as a volunteer preparing for the bazaar opening with her usual enthusiasm, could get into the not yet opened bazaar with no problem. Randy and I had not slept for twenty eight hours; Randy went to bed. Patti and I walked to the Officers Club to see the bazaar.

When we walked inside, I stood breathless looking at sparkling lights reflecting off lines of tables laden with crystal objects, Dresden china, Barbarian china, delicate figurines, Italian ceramics, and Venetian glass. Everywhere were green Christmas trees beautifully decorated with hand made colorful ornaments. Directly in front of me were the famous Christmas angels from Nuremberg with delicate faces of wax and elegant velvet gowns with gold trim. I knew I wanted one for the top of my artificial Christmas tree in Riyadh! Next to these were all sizes and sorts of German candles, and at a table across from the candles were the loveliest handmade tree decorations I have ever seen. In the next room were paintings, Goebel and Hummel figurines, nativity scenes, brass from Holland, brass from Iran, Persian carpets, pewter items, woolen plaid skirts from England, English bone china, wooden Christmas tree decorations, other decorations of all kinds, colorful handmade puppets from England, and many more items from many countries. We traveled from Saudi Arabia to this early celebration of Christmas. It was almost too much! We spent three days at the bazaar and memorized every item of interest in order to make our selection. If a prize had been given for those who traveled the furthest to shop the bazaar, we would have won. Our reputation spread throughout the bazaar. People found it hard to believe that we came from Saudi Arabia just to visit this bazaar!

Afterwards, Patti, Randy, and I took the train to Florence, Italy. Sarina flew back to Saudi with friends so she would not miss more school. Our train left in the wee hours of the morning. We entered the first sleeping compartment with available beds. We were surprised to find men in our compartment. Of course, they paid us no attention; but we did not realize that men and women share sleeping compartments. Each compartment sleeps six people and it's simply first come, first serve. It was hard to believe that we departed Saudi Arabia just days ago where married men and women do not mix in public and now we were sleeping with strange men. What an interesting world!

ME WITH RANDY IN TIRRENIA, ITALY

The next morning we awoke early. Randy, who slept with her boots on all night for extra protection from our compartment neighbors, now had swollen feet. Being the humorist that she is, her remarks about strange men and swollen feet that looked as if gangrene had set in, had us in stitches. I do not know how Randy did it, but she always had the right word for the right moment! We were in good spirits and happy to be going to Florence to sight see and to change trains and head for Tirrenia to visit Camp Darby friends. Both Patti and I had relocated to Saudi from Tirrenia where Chet and Joe had worked together. Randy, who knew Tirrenia only through our stories, was looking forward to meeting friends. All of us were happy that we would be able to attend the chapel at Camp Darby for Sunday Protestant services and Catholic mass. The Protestant minister was a friend of mine, and the Catholic priest was a friend of Patti's.

After sightseeing in Florence, we took the train to Pisa and a taxi to Tirrenia. The tree lined streets were inviting; tall pine trees were everywhere. Once more, I saw the scenes of Italy that brought back such wonderful memories. When we first arrived in Italy in 1973, five year old Preston, who had lived in several different countries, exclaimed, "This is the best world yet!" How right he was about Italy. It is a country with a lot of love. I saw the familiar scenes of old men and women going to market on their bicycles or motor scooters. We passed through the little town of Marina de Pisa, picturesque with its small farms and neat stone houses. As a matter of fact, stone walls are all over Italy and date back to the time of the Romans and earlier. I thought about our high wall in Saudi and reminisced a bit about "walls." I suppose people always have built walls to establish boundaries and to keep people out. The real truth about walls is that they keep people inside, imprisoning lives. How many wars have been fought because someone crossed a boundary and enraged people on the other side of the boundary. How much misunderstanding exists from one country to the next because countries have closed themselves in, rather than forming intelligent relationships to bridge misunderstanding. The desert Bedouin locked itself solidly into the desert for four thousand years. Even after the Islamic wars, Bedouin warriors retreated back into the desert and into an ancient way of life. Proud and defiant, they wanted no one else.

Even today, I believe the Saudis could walk away from expensive cars and houses, mount up on camels, and lose themselves, once more, in the desert. Entering the global energy marketplace has forced them to build business relationships, but even these, I believe are superficial. Like an abusive husband who beats his wife, Saudi has much to hid from outsiders. Unfortunately, Saudi uses the US to build their status in the Middle East. They fear Iraq, their neighbors to the north, but I can imagine that Iraq, a country where civilization likely began and that educates men and women, envisions Saudi as their illiterate religious neighbor with money. To make matters worse, Iraq's offensive neighbor has bought itself a powerful uncle. Today, the US is building King Khaled Military City near the Iraqi border to protect Saudi Arabia and is ensuring that Saudi is well armed. It is only a matter of time before Saudi turns against the US. I fear that, one day, the US will have a dear price to pay for plentiful, inexpensive oil.

The Golf Hotel, named for its golf course, in the delightful Mediterranean town of Tirrenia, was to be our home for the next several days. The massive lobby with its polished marble floors looked clean and cold! Sensible Italians, like all Europeans, have been conserving energy since the oil embargo of 1973; they refuse to turn the heat on until November, regardless of cold weather. It was the early part of November, and we wondered if we would have heat! We could not leave Saudi completely behind us. The problem of oil stretched its ugly fingers out around the globe.

The hotel clerk was happy to see us and remembered us from our stay here while we waited to go to Saudi Arabia after moving out of our houses. He asked us about Saudi Arabia, but he refused to believe any of our stories! Actually, no one believed our stories about Saudi. We had been out of Saudi for five days, and many people questioned us. No one could believe our stories about walled compounds, black-veiled women, and Head Choppers Square. We went to our rooms on the third floor; they were warm! Hurray! It felt good to be warm. We had been without heat on the train. Europeans were diligent in conserving heat. Only Americans have had the luxury of such inexpensive heat for so long. Europeans drove small cars and wore warm woolen clothing while Americans still wore polyester! Europeans stay fit by walking to the train or bus station, walking to work, to school, and to the marketplace; they are not fat! Also, bicycles are a major part of the transportation system. I believe such daily exercise contributes to their gregarious nature and their creative energy.

Our five days in Italy was refreshing for each of us. It was good to see old friends who were surprised to see Patti and me. They looked at us as if we had returned from the grave! When we left Camp Darby for Saudi Arabia, they thought we would never be heard from again. Our chaplain, Reverend Woods, had preached a series of sermons especially for those of us going to Saudi. His Biblical texts had been taken from Colossians because the little church in Colosse was in a far away and difficult to reach location. Paul, the author of Colossians, had concern for the little church. Reverend Woods sermons were built around verses such as, "For this cause, we also, since the day we heard, do not cease to pray for you and to desire that you might be filled with the knowledge of his will in all wisdom and all spiritual understanding: that you might walk worthy of the Lord unto all pleasing, being fruitful in all good work, and increasing in the knowledge of God: strengthened with all might, according to his glorious power, unto all patience and long-suffering with joyfulness: Giving thanks to the father, which hath made us to be partakers of the inheritance of the saints in light; who hath delivered us from the power of darkness, and hath translated us into the kingdom of his dear Son." When the Camp Darby families began leaving for Saudi Arabia, Chaplain Woods felt a real sorrow as he watched one family after another depart. Finally, many families left and only a small congregation was left behind. The military buildup in Saudi left this base drained of families who were active in many areas of life at the base and surrounding it.

Sunday evening, after arriving in Tirrenia and unpacking, I was in church again. How good it was! Chaplain Woods asked me to tell about Saudi Arabia, and I tried to describe it; but it was difficult to explain. Here in Italy, in this chapel at Camp Darby, I was a million light years away from Saudi Arabia. The next day as we walked around Tirrenia, my heart went out to Preston who left such freedom behind. I cried when I came to the tree-lined street where we once lived. I could picture Preston on his bike playing with his friends, and Julie running behind him. I wanted to return to life as it had been in Tirrenia, without the dust, dirt, flies, and very strange people of Saudi Arabia. Patti also enjoyed our Tirrenia visit; she was happy to see Father Mertz and other friends. Several evenings during our visit, we enjoyed excellent Italian restaurants with Father Mertz, a connoisseur of Italian food. In Saudi there were few places to eat, so eating out in Tirrenia was a treat for us!

Soon our time was up, and the time to return to Riyadh was at hand. On the airplane from Rome to Riyadh, we reminisced about our experiences and about our purchases! It was hard to leave so much behind us. Now we were entering a dark tunnel; we were about to be transformed back into time thousands of years ago. We were going to a place where my own faith was unlawful and virtually unknown. Saudi was a place of darkness; as the plane hurled us toward our destination, I prayed for survival strength.

CHAPTER FIVE -- MY DESERT ROUTINE
Riyadh, Saudi Arabia – 1977

The Sands of Time – ruins in the Saudi desert

Soon we were back in Riyadh and in the routine of things. We always were up early in the morning. Preston had to catch his bus for school at seven in the morning. The school bus bumped Preston and his friends all over the desert as it went from one lonely compound to another. Once, Sarina came home complaining that the top of her head hurt because the bus driver hit a big bump in the road and all the passengers hit the roof of the bus. Bumpy rides were not unusual. The inquisitive and outgoing Yemen and Ethiopian drivers enjoyed driving while talking with passengers. Once Patti and I were in a small bus returning from the commissary where we purchased groceries. Our driver, who was expounding great knowledge of President Carter, suddenly came down a hill with the speed of a roller coaster as Patti and I lifted completely off our seats and found ourselves in mid-air. The experience was stunning. We were silent for a moment, and then Patti and I began laughing at our own shocked expressions. That afternoon when Sarina came home from school, we sympathized with her school bus tales.

One frightening afternoon, the school bus transporting Preston and Anela failed to come home at all. Patti and I waited all afternoon and told one another that everything was all right. We had no way to find out. When Joe and Chet came home from work, Preston and Anela were with them. They told us that the bus driver could not find our compound and finally took these two, tired, hot, thirsty children to one of the Corps offices. Remarkably, Preston and Anela survived without harm and seemed untouched by the situation. They, too, were learning to take things in stride; nothing seemed to surprise them. They told us they tired to show the driver where they lived, but he spoke little English and could not understand them.

In the desert, my days began with killing flies in our kitchen, especially on the kitchen window which faced the direction of the morning sun and was the first place to warm up in the mornings. The flies loved that window! They were able to get inside the house because each day flies swarmed on the front doors and on the windows. Always, during the day, some would manage to get inside. The next morning, they could be found congregated on my kitchen window. Usually, I would kill twenty or thirty, then sweep them into a pile and put them in the trash. Also, the mouse trap had to be emptied. That was Chet's job. Sometimes our mouse trap would contain a cute little mouse that looked as if it should be in a pet shop window.

In the desert, eye diseases are common because it is difficult to brush pesky flies away. Adults or children who spend considerable time outside are at risk. Flies are starved for moisture; and they will go to ears, eyes, mouth or to an open wound to get moisture. Therefore disease is rampant. It is not unusual to see Saudi children with flies caked around the eyes and mouth. Flies stick to children and refuse to go away. Children get used to them and eventually do not try to swat at them. In a place that is moisture starved, water is precious; many desert people do not bathe often and cleanliness becomes a problem.

As more Westerners arrive in Saudi, there are more medical facilities. The new King Khaled Military Hospital, with its American and British doctors, has modern equipment and it well staffed. I am told that, because King Khaled has heart disease and because congenital heart disease is prevalent throughout Saudi, there is a modern cardiac floor staffed with well-known surgical teams. There are other hospitals in Riyadh staffed with Egyptian, Lebanese, or Pakistani doctors. However, one huge problem faced by Saudi officials is that of overcoming superstition. Many Saudis believe that disease is the will of Allah, and they will not utilize medical facilities even though medical care is free to the Saudis. I am so thankful for my own Western heritage and my faith. Where knowledge flourished, science made important discoveries in medicine, technology, geology, space exploration, and so many other areas. However, Christianity has its own dark side, and I know it is imperative that I have respect for other people's faith; religion throughout the world must become more about love and understanding and less about hate.

SARINA, ME, CHET JUST BEFORE A TRIP HOME

Chet and Preston and I flew home to Jacksonville to meet Allen for Christmas. Our home in North Shore on the Chesapeake Bay in Maryland was rented; Florida was the place to go to be with family. Always it was fun to be with my mother and my sister

Grace and her friends Dorsey and Lynette. Sometimes my other sister Debra, who lived in a different state, would come for a visit. All of us enjoyed discussing world events and about what God was doing in local Jacksonville churches. Allen and Preston sometimes sat in on our discussions, listened intently, and joined in with us. My mother and father attended Southside Assembly of God Church where Pastor Zinc taught the virtues of living a holy life. My dad, an alcoholic for many years, stopped drinking and became a brand new person. It was awesome. Chet was happy visiting in Jacksonville with his family. He and his mother are close and enjoy seeing one another. He especially enjoys his mom's cooking, and she fills up her kitchen with all the foods he enjoys. Chet and I both enjoy long hours spent with our good friends, Gail and John Goode. Gail and John, Florida home builders and world travelers, are our long-time best friends. While we lived in Italy, they built a beautiful home on the St. Johns River in Jacksonville -- perfect for having guests and entertaining. During our Jacksonville visits, we always spend evenings together, eating, laughing, storytelling, and having a great time!

On the way back to Saudi, we saw the Arcari family in the London airport. We all hugged and said, "Oh no!" about going back to Saudi. For me, the Saudi experience begins at the London airport while in line to board the airplane for Riyadh. Saudia Airlines has an airline hub in London where many Saudis have homes and investments. London is my cross-over point from a modern world to an ancient world. Standing in the airport, I now was encircled by black-veiled women holding onto babies and small children, along with tired looking men from many countries. At 2 a.m. we arrived tired and hungry in Riyadh. We drove to our desert compound and found dust and dirt covering everything, a sign that dust storms had passed through Riyadh while we were in the States. A dust storm is a desert wind storm that picks up tons of sand and debris, infiltrating every nook and cranny of every building with grainy dust and sand particles. The grimy sand was on my countertops, inside my closed cabinets on my dishes, on our beds, on our carpets, and just everywhere! Cleaning up after a dust storm is a big job! What a sight to face! In the midst of the dust, a mouse was running back and forth across the kitchen counter. The Arcari's walked into our house to see if it looked any better than their house, and I offered to make hot tea to cheer us up. I turned on the stove burner but nothing happened. In the midst of energy-rich Saudi Arabia, we were out of gas for the stove! Suddenly, Chet grabbed a broom and started chasing a mouse. A crashing sound filled the house as the broom missed the mouse and came crashing down, breaking a grimy glass. It was too much! We all started to laugh. It was either laugh or cry! The next day, Randy and Jackie came over to welcome us back to our desert home. I was in no mood to hear them! Probably, I was rude. Later, I apologized to them. How could I have been so terrible to them? While we were Stateside, they endured a lonely, quiet Christmas with sandstorms. Each of them vowed they would never again spend another Christmas in Saudi!

Within a few days, I was fine and back in the swing of things. The human spirit is so adaptable! It always amazed me that, once back in Saudi, I could adapt once more to my desert life. I now was working part time for Revlon Cosmetics. During my previous Italy visit, my former boss Ernie Trostle, asked if I would order Revlon into Saudi through the US military exchange. I agreed and soon Moon Drops Moisturizing products, Charlie fragrances, and Revlon hair spray appeared on the shelves of the Riyadh exchange. I had many happy customers. I also ordered products for US exchanges in Jeddah and Dhahran. I worked previously with Revlon in the Far East and in Europe with no particular problems. Saudi was different. My product delivery pipeline was New York to Frankfurt to Saudi Arabia. In Frankfurt, of course, the military gave no special shipment priority to my products. Consequently, my cosmetic shipments backed up in warehouses in Frankfurt. No Revlon Christmas products arrived in Saudi. Finally, Christmas deliveries arrived in the spring along with several months worth of monthly orders. Thousands of dollars of merchandise had to be opened, itemized, priced, put on shelves, and sold. I had a mountain of merchandise sitting in the desert in Riyadh and in Dhahran. I feared the Saudis would hang me by my painted toenails!

Chet didn't seem worried about the matter. He said Saudis are good about such matters as cosmetics, as long as the situation is not a real irritant. I wondered if a mountain of Moon Drops product could qualify as an irritant to the Saudis. I tried to open products as quickly as possible, even as perfumes exploded in my face in the 120 degree weather. Both store managers were ready for my head; if the Saudis didn't get me, the store managers might; my products were taking up their warehouse space and spilling over into the desert. There were mounds and mounds of boxes. Some days Patti would come with me to the exchange and stand out in the sun and the dust to help unpack items. After several weeks, I would get on the plane for Dhahran and open their merchandise. It was a nightmare. Somehow, after several months, I managed to get through the mountain and get the products on the shelves. I never ordered cosmetics into Saudi again.

While flying back and forth to Dhahran, I had interesting experiences. Generally, I was the only women flying alone in a plane full of men; I guess I was a bit of a novelty. Once, when returning to Riyadh from Dhahran, I sat next to a black-veiled woman. I paid no attention to her and assumed the response would be the same. Suddenly, she jerked off her veil and said to me, "I am so tired of wearing this thing; I hate it!" I was shocked and speechless. She looked to be about seventeen years of age. She told me her life story which lasted the entire one hour flight.

She said she was born in Riyadh to wealthy Saudi parents. Her father was an important officer in the Saudi military. When she was twelve, her parents divorced and she went to live with her mother and her four siblings in London where she went to school and became westernized. Now, her father insisted that she return to Saudi to live and become a loyal citizen if she wanted to receive her large inheritance. Her other siblings graduated from schools in London and, one by one, returned to Riyadh to live with their father. Now it was her turn, and she was frantic. Her brothers did not mind returning and working with their father, but she was the youngest child who loved western ways and never wanted to return. She never wanted to give up her freedom; she did not know what to do. On the plane, she had put the veil on for the first time. My heart went out to her! As we landed in Riyadh, she began putting the veil on once more. She told me she hated the Saudi royal family and she hated Riyadh. She said if she tried to escape, go to America, lead a normal life, and marry an American, that her father would have her killed.

When we arrived at the terminal, Chet was not there to meet me. Later, I realized he had the wrong arrival time. Strangely, her brother was not there to meet her. She was frightened and looked as if she would cry. I pointed to a public phone and suggested that she call her brother. She replied that, as a veiled woman, she was not allowed to make phone calls. (Religious public policy declared this for Saudi women, fearing that they might call a man.) I could not believe such a hindrance for anyone. I took the number of her brother and called him for her. An older sister answered the phone and said the brother was on his way. Soon a black Mercedes arrived and a man in his late twenties got out and walked toward us. It was her brother. Chet had not yet arrived, so the brother offered to take me home. During the drive through Riyadh, I noticed the young woman looking nervously out the car window. What a strange incident to witness! I learned that the brother and his father owned a construction business. I thought he and Chet might like to meet one another. Meanwhile I was trying to console his poor sister who was being ignored by him.

No one at my compound knew we were on the way. When we arrived at the gate, I rang the bell and Patti opened the gate. She and Joe were leaving for an evening military event, and Patti was wearing a long, low cut gown that was fashionable and modest by American standards. However, when she saw me with a Saudi man and woman, her hands went to her upper half as she tried to cover up! It would have been a hilarious scene if it had not been such a serious moment. I introduced them; Patti tried to shake hands and cover up all at once. We went to my front door and Chet answered the door. He, too, was surprised. I offered to make tea for everyone. The brother and the woman stayed for awhile. Chet, a civil engineer, enjoyed meeting them and enjoyed the conversation. The brother came to see Chet several times afterwards at Chet's office. The young women never came to see me again. A year later, Chet and I saw the brother and an older sister in a grocery shop. I asked about the younger sister and was told that she was adjusting to Riyadh; it was made clear that she would not be allowed to visit me. I remembered that, on the plane, she said she would be in Saudi only a few months. My impression was that she was a hostage of her own family.

UNVEILINGS
A Desert Journey
by
Patricia Adora Clark Taylor

CHAPTER SIX -- EXPANDING HORIZONS
Riyadh, Saudi Arabia -- 1977

1977 -- Downtown Riyadh with Light Poles

Even while the cosmetics business was keeping me busy, I was approached by Dr. Woodberry and Roberta about having a women's Bible study group at my house once a week during the day. It would be a time for women to come together for study and to share their experiences. I agreed and drew a map to my house which was distributed at the Friday morning church meeting. The hand drawn map was crude, and I doubted that anyone would find me in my isolated compound.

In January of 1977, the first women's study group met at my house. Patti baked a cake and brought it over for us. As far as I know, each woman who set out that day to come to the meeting was successful in getting there. The women began arriving, one by one. Some came with only their drivers; some came with three or four other women. Some found the compound immediately, some rode around in the desert for awhile before their drivers found the location. Sixteen women comprised that first meeting; later the meetings grew to about forty. We began with mostly American women, but as the meetings grew, women from different countries attended and joined the discussions. In the two years that followed, we studied and prayed together. It was an exciting group, and we looked forward to those meetings!

I remember the meetings and the individuals vividly. Roberta could expound on any subject with her wealth of knowledge from university study in Beirut, life in Kabul as a missionary, and extensive middle east travel. One woman came from the States with her two young daughters and her American archeologist husband who was excavating ancient gold mines on the east coast of Saudi. Her husband, employed by the Saudi Arabian government, had no significant American alliances; his wife had been lonely and needed friends. One day, while she was at the market place in Riyadh where they lived, she ran into a high school friend. She was so surprised! Her friend told her that she had become a Christian and was a changed person. The friend shared her own story and spoke about Jesus. The result was that the woman, and her archeologist husband, became Christians. This young American woman with two little girls found her way to the Bible study and was a great addition. Later, her husband shared with us about Saudi Arabia's history and the latest archeology discoveries. He said there was a theory that the mines currently under excavation in Saudi Arabia were King Solomon's gold mines. Later, the archeologist and his family returned to the States, where he was a university professor; we later heard that he was teaching a Sunday School class. Another woman, delightfully English and very well traveled, was knowledgeable about the scriptures and middle east history and shared many of her own experiences.

Every woman had a story to tell about how she came to Saudi Arabia and how she arrived at my compound. For each of us, it had been a long journey; but God was with us. During those meetings we prayed together, oh how we prayed! We prayed for ourselves and for our families. We prayed for safety and for God's blessings. We prayed for blessings for Saudi Arabia and for all its people. We prayed that a time of renewal and awakening would come to this desert land. Once we were visited by a Lebanese minister and his wife. They now lived in Bahrain, an island off the east coast of Saudi Arabia. They said to us, "When women pray, great things happen." We all knew it was true. They related to us that groups like ours were coming together all over Saudi Arabia and were praying for this country. We were privileged to be part of what God was doing in Saudi Arabia.

Every evening before bed, Preston and I prayed together. He was a strong prayer partner. We prayed for everyone and everything that came to mind. We prayed for safety for our compound's people and for Julie and Bruce. I know it worked. Once Julie escaped from our compound and did not return for an hour. We had been warned to keep our animals inside because wild desert dogs roamed the area of our compound. At night, we could hear them barking and howling. Finally, Julie returned with her tail wagging and ran into the compound. She was so proud; she brought three desert dogs home with her. I opened the front door; Julie ran inside. The large desert dogs relaxed comfortably on my front porch for several hours; then left and never returned. After that, I knew Julie would survive Saudi; and she did and lived for many years!

A young Ethiopian man came to my gate one day. He spoke perfect English and wanted to know if his sister could come to live with us as our housekeeper. He and his sister came to Saudi from Ethiopia; both had been sponsored into the country by members of the Saudi royal family. Both were Christians; their father had been head of their village in Ethiopia where he made education available for girls and boys. He had been killed in recent uprisings; his two children escaped to Saudi. I told the man that my husband and I would discuss the idea of his sister staying with us. That evening Chet and I agreed that I should meet her. The next day Mobra came to see me. I liked her right away. She looked to be about sixteen and was small and shy with a beautiful smile. I walked her though the house and showed her the bedroom that would be hers. I could tell that she was delighted even though she spoke very little. She stayed with us for about six months, and I could see that she longed to return to her home and to life as it had been in Ethiopia. One day I saw her staring out the window. She told me that she missed Ethiopia's green trees and her quiet village, and she missed her father. She knew she would never return to life as it had been before the destruction. She and her brother wanted to go to the United States where he might study medicine. One day her brother came for her and said it was time for them to move on to one of the coastal cities. It is my hope that they were able to make their dreams come true.

During the time I knew these two beautiful Ethiopian people, I wanted to help them in some significant way. I wanted to write someone somewhere who could help. I did not know what would be helpful. In the end, I did nothing. Now I do not know where they are and what will happen to them. They have no home to return to; no place to go. How sad it is!

America is such a fortunate country. So many homeless, tired, and hungry refugees want to get to America. When I see refugees, I think, "There but for the grace of God, go I." I remember refugees in Amman, Jordan living in cardboard boxes. Here in Saudi, there are many, many refugees living in large cardboard boxes. For instance, a large box once containing a refrigerator is now a now a make-shift home. Third world nations are filled with refugees traveling from one place of upheaval to another. Throughout the middle east, poverty, disease, and death live next door to opulent wealth. Is it possible that the United States is protected; is it possible that it truly is safe? When I return to the quiet beauty of my peaceful Maryland home on the Magothy River, all of this will seem like a dream and no one will believe my stories. I keep notes because even I will wonder if it was my imagination.

In Saudi, Chet and I met an Egyptian couple at church. They attended both the Arabic and English services where they often were greeters at the door. Each of them had intelligent, smiling faces, and outgoing personalities. He was a physician; she was an accountant. We were delighted when they invited us for dinner at their apartment. When we arrived, I was surprised to see how meagerly they lived. The small, orderly apartment was inexpensively furnished. Immediately we were drawn into lively conversation and later enjoyed a superb Egyptian meal with fresh vegetable and meat dishes and fruit for desert. They told us about being Christians in Egypt and how their lifestyle revolved around their Christian meetings. I asked them how they knew about Jesus, and they looked surprised. Their answer, "Don't you remember that Jesus came to live in Egypt when he was a baby? In Egypt, Jesus was safe; we always have known about Jesus." Later, when we had them over for dinner one evening, it was with the usual crystal, china, and silver that we always use for entertaining. Trying to reconcile the differences in our living standards was difficult for me. Americans are just so wealthy compared to people of other countries.

Our Egyptian friends, also, wanted to come to the United States one day. Many Egyptians are the educated elite of the Middle East, but they must travel to other countries to make a living. They work hard, keep a good attitude, and often send money back home to support relatives. Many times, it is the educated elite who leave to find a better life. Previously, when visiting Taiwan, I met many educated Chinese Christians who fled China's Mao Tse Tung regime and became Taiwan Chinese. They told me they would have been killed if they remained in China. In violent upheavals, educated intellectuals are the first to be removed as a way of "cleansing" the population.

In February of 1977, I took my first trip to Jeddah, a seacoast city on the west coast of Saudi Arabia filled with history. Its nomadic people long have been linked by the Red Sea to Mediterranean nations such as Israel, Egypt, Jordan, Lebanon, Iran, Iraq, Syria, and many other nations. Caravans traveled throughout this region transporting expensive spices such as frankincense and myrrh which come from the south of Saudi Arabia and are necessary for embalming and burial procedures. It is believed that the Queen of Sheba lived south of Jeddah in the city of Sheba about 900 BC and controlled these powerful trade routes. She likely would have gone to King Solomon seeking protection for her influential and profitable trade routes. Mohammed was born along this western coast about 571 AD He traveled up and down this coast and camped with people in Christian and Jewish settlements and from many parts of the world. Mohammed observed the discipline of the Christian and Jewish settlements, and had respect for their "book." He referred to them as "people of the book." He learned many of the Old Testament stories, and he learned about Jesus. He wanted his own people, also, to be people of the book. Finally, he wrote the Koran (western spelling) or Qu'ran (eastern spelling).

The book that emerged is a book of law encompassing every area of life. It is not surprising that Mohammed wrote such a book since desert people traditionally have been known for their wisdom and strict law. Some scholars think the book of Job reflects the wisdom of northwest Arabia. Also, the last two books of Proverbs may have been written by Arabians. The Koran is written in prose and reads likes Psalms or Proverbs. One of the verses concerning Saudi Arabia reads, "Thus we appoint a midmost nation that you might be witnesses to the people, and that the Messenger might be a witness to you. Turn thy face toward the Holy Mosque; and wherever you are, turn your faces toward it." (Holy Koran II.) The Holy Mosque in the passage is in this "midmost nation" of Saudi Arabia where Mecca is located south of Jeddah.

While in Jeddah, I visited with friends and was happy to be where the air was humid and where there were trees and green grass. The greenery of Jeddah looked good to me, and all in all, Jeddah provided a delightful change for a few days. One evening my friends took me to a recreation area on the Red Sea that was managed by the Corps of Engineers.

We had a steak dinner outside on the patio as the wind blew off the Red Sea. Just to be near a body of water again was refreshing! That night and throughout my visit, people told me of the region's earliest history. I was told that an ancient monument to Eve existed near Jeddah and dated back thousands of years. At the time, I remember thinking how funny that seemed. I wanted to laugh out loud. The very thought of Eve and the Garden of Eden as being anywhere near Saudi seemed ludicrous! However, if Adam and Eve lived for a thousand years, they would have gotten around quite a bit. Who knows where they might have traveled? The holy site at Mecca was supposed to have been visited by Adam. If the Garden of Eden was in the area of Palestine, and Adam and Eve were banished to the east, they could have stayed along the coast of Saudi Arabia for a time. Within a thousand years, Adam and Eve could have traveled from Palestine to Saudi Arabia and on to the area of the Tigris and Euphrates rivers in modern day Iraq. Years later, Abraham left Iraq's ancient city of Ur and set out for the Jordan River Valley area. The second chapter of Genesis tells about the land of Havilah which some believe to be near the ancient site of Mecca, an age old site considered sacred even before the faith of Islam.

Shopping in Jeddah was more fun than in Riyadh because I didn't feel as confined being a woman. The coastal area is more international and laws are not as strictly enforced as in Riyadh. Therefore jeans or a skirt that came below the knees certainly was acceptable. In Riyadh, I always felt that a long skirt to the ankles should be worn, although I have worn shorter skirts. Even so, I was reminded of the horror stories of the motawa (religious police) with their cans of paint, who would come up to women and spray their ankles and legs with red spray paint if women dared show these body parts! The stories stuck in my mind, but I never saw this happen; it seems the motawa have given up since so many women have come to Saudi Arabia from all over the world! Long skirts are hard to wear in Riyadh due to the difficulty of stepping over and around rocks, stones, building debris, holes in the road, etc. Carrying packages only added to the problem. In Jeddah, it actually was fun to shop, and I was more relaxed winding through the old and new suqs with their unusual items from around the world.

The fall and spring of 1977 passed quickly. Jackie was involved with her job and enjoying her work. Randy was busy with school children with runny noses, scratches and bruises, and occasional broken bones. Patti was busy cooking delicious Italian meals and having celebrations for every occasion. Never was a birthday or a holiday overlooked. When Patti went with Sarina to Europe once a month, they returned with whatever was needed for a special celebration. Meanwhile, I was in lipstick and perfume up to my ears, so we all kept busy. It was a good time in my life; more than that, it was a special time. Each of us had adapted well. Our confidence grew as we learned our way around the city; we, also, insisted that our drivers drive with more caution. In airports, we were asserting ourselves. When a Saudi man pushed us aside and stepped in front of us, we stepped back into our rightful place while signaling to an airline official that we were being mistreated. We were getting good results. It was a worthwhile lesson for each of us, and we were being treated with more respect.

At home there was, of course, no television; and I was reading whenever I had spare time. Chet was reading lengthy novels, and I was reading about Saudi history and culture and about Islam, Christianity, and Judaism. Particularly, I was interested in the Bedouin way of life. I acquired a book about the desert camel culture which explained the relationship between desert people and their camels. The book revealed how each was dependent on the other. The desert nomadic lifestyle strictly revolved around the unique ability of the camel to go long distances without water, to transport people or goods, and to provide milk Camels even provide fellowship with their own brand of humor and their stubbornness. I read about one Bedouin who knew to take off his headdress each morning and let his camel stomp on it before the camel would began a day's work! I was surprised to read that pregnant camels have difficult deliveries because of the long, spindly legs of the baby camel; many camels would die giving birth if it were not for human hands to help in the delivery. Camels are highly prized; a Bedouin with strong, healthy camels can be the equivalent of a millionaire.

I had a growing interest in the effect of religion on culture, particularly on education. The Saudis seemed uneducated, backward, irresponsible, and disorganized. Saudis had no great love for Americans; although Americans were well paid, it was clear that we were the worker bees hired to do their bidding. Those of us who came under the American military umbrella were protected from the most brutal Saudi treatment given to foreign workers. Much more vulnerable were individuals working directly for the Saudis. Punishment could be cruel if they stepped out of line in any way. While in Saudi I heard stories about two British workers being flogged in public for having alcohol. On the other hand, the Corps of Engineers office once received a call from Saudi officials stating that their "furniture" had arrived and was leaking on the dock. Actually, the monthly shipment of crates of alcohol had arrived and some broken bottles were leaking from containers. In Saudi I saw more alcohol consumed than when we lived in Italy. A monthly shipment came into the country crated for Corps personnel. Johnny Walker was a real favorite!

Notes: *In spite of such special treatment, I believe the Saudis had a particular dislike for Americans whom they must have viewed as the premier oil addicts of the world. Why would anyone think that the Saudis liked us! They used our educated work force and our expertise to build their country. At the same time, they used American petrodollars to fund their opulent lifestyle for an expanding "royal family" while giving away just enough to keep the masses quiet and funding whatever "charities" or programs of interest to them. America had no interest in how our petrodollars were spent. There was no plan for educating the masses to become independent citizens capable of rational thought. Such a notion would be seen as a threat to the iron grip of the royal family who made concessions to strict religious leaders.*

American policy was to keep the Saudis happy while refusing to develop alternative fuels. Many Americans thought it was a real bargain. Our American dollars went into Saudi petroleum banks and were used for whatever the Saudis desired; it occurred to me that one day these American petrodollars might be turned back on Americans. In the late 1970s, President Carter, who understood the danger of our energy policy, wisely initiated an "alternative fuels initiative" which was dismantled in the decade of the 80s during President Reagan's presidency. By the end of the 1980s, disastrous American policies resulted in a Gulf War and a nearly bankrupt US. Only American arms dealers were thrilled; they made a fortune arming Saudi Arabia with modern weapons, aircraft, and war technologies. During the 1990s, it was petroleum business as usual. By the time the new millennium arrived, Saudi terrorists were crashing into American buildings.

UNVEILINGS
A Desert Journey
by
Patricia Adora Clark Taylor

CHAPTER SEVEN -- CHANGING TIMES
Riyadh, Saudi Arabia -- 1977

1977– Chet and Preston in Wadi Hanifa Date Grove

Preston's spring break came in April of 1977, and we decided to meet Patti, Joe, Sarina and Anela in Italy where they would be vacationing. Chet was unable to get away from work, but he encouraged us to go. He knew that Preston, in particular, needed the break; he bought our tickets and took us to the airport. Traveling with us was a little Italian woman who was the mother of one of the women who worked with Chet. The woman asked if I would escort her mother home to Livorno, and I was happy to oblige. The mother spoke no English, so it was a chance for me to practice my Italian. We flew, first of all, to the airport in Jeddah where we had a connecting flight to Rome. When we arrived in Jeddah, the airport was filled with persons leaving the country because it was a Wednesday night, the beginning of the weekend when many of the workers try to leave for a few days. Also, it was near Easter; and most likely, Christian workers were leaving for vacation. The airport was jammed with crowds of people -- all men. I think the little Italian woman and I were the only females. For about an hour the three of us stood among crowds of people; we were unable to get near the ticket counter which by now had been completely overturned by the pushing throngs of people.

Finally, a well dressed gentleman come over to me and asked if he could help the three of us. I recognized him as having been on the flight from Riyadh. He said he had a friend who was a Saudia Airlines official and could get us boarding passes for the flight to Europe. Since I didn't know what else to do, I handed him our tickets and passports which he promptly took, then returned with everything in order. He ushered us into the dingy lounge filled with people; he found us a seat and ordered us orange drinks. We certainly were grateful! He said he would be on our flight, but that he would be traveling on to Paris. I assumed he was French. However, when we passed through the last checkpoint area and showed our passports, I saw that he was a Saudi. I was shocked that this man could be both civilized and Saudi! When we arrived in Rome, he did not leave us until he made sure that we would have no problem with our connecting flight to Livorno. That incident restored my faith in Saudi humanity.

Late that afternoon, we arrived safely in the little town of Tirrenia at the Golf Hotel to see Patti and Joe and their girls. The next day Preston went to his former school on the army base; he walked into the cafeteria at lunch time and surprised his classmates. His teacher let him attend classes with his friends and Preston was able to answer many questions about Saudi Arabia. I think he actually enjoyed giving exciting accounts of his life in Saudi including stories about his international school in Riyadh, his friends from around the world, and daily desert compound life! All in all it was a great vacation. Preston breathed in the gentle Mediterranean air and visited familiar places; he proved to be a great traveling buddy!

When we returned to Riyadh, we knew it would not be long until summer when we would spend two months in the States. Patti and Joe received news that they were being transferred early out of Saudi to Heidelberg, Germany. They were thrilled, and all of us in the compound were happy for them even though we would miss them! When I heard the news, I thought, "What will I ever do without my friend Patti?" In May, Randy, Jackie and I had an international dinner party at our compound as a farewell to Patti and Joe and the girls. We acquired a huge Bedouin tent from a friend and raised it up in the yard. Inside the massive tent, we put tables lined with delicious assortments of foods prepared by us and brightly burning candles in candle holders from different parts of the world. We invited a musical Italian friend living in Saudi, who invented and constructed his own portable organ, to join us and provide the music. He was a hit at parties with his lively, fun music that suddenly could become soft and romantic! Eighty guests attended, and we danced and danced! Friends brought an assortment of bathtub, homemade wine and other beverages. Some people even ordered bottles and made their own labels! What an evening under the stars in the midst of the desert in Saudi Arabia!

That summer, Preston was ready for another break from behind concrete walls. Allen, still in school in the States, wanted to leave the States for the summer and take a summer job in Riyadh to make money for stereo equipment and other items for his room at school. Rarely did Chet get a break from his work, so Chet and I decided that I would take Preston to the States, and he would stay in Saudi with Allen. When Allen arrived in Riyadh we all met him and had a few great days together. Then Preston and I left for Florida. Allen quickly secured a job working in the Corps of Engineers' Riyadh mail room; and, with his big strong build, was able to load and unload large bags of mail. Allen accompanied the mail driver around town when mail was picked up and delivered, and he enjoyed the job's mobility. Allen also was happy to be with many other Corps of Engineer's teenagers who were home for the summer. The Saudis insisted that foreign students, beginning in ninth grade, go away to school; but the students were allowed to join their families in Saudi for the summer and for holidays. Apparently the Saudi government decided there were enough problems trying to reconcile an ancient culture to western civilization without having to deal, all year long, with teenage energy and hormone levels.

Preston and I traveled to Germany and stayed for a few days with Patti and Joe and the girls and helped them move into their new quarters in Heidelberg. They had taken time to travel throughout southern Europe and were ready to settle into their latest home. We all enjoyed laughing and talking about times past. Finally, the day arrived when Preston and I left for the States. During the long flight, I stared out the airplane window for hours and looked at the blue sky high above the ocean. I was happy to be going home to Florida, but I was feeling the loss of Patti and Joe from my Saudi home. After my Stateside vacation, I would face another year in Saudi without them. Even then, the God of the universe was making plans and preparing the way.

The time at home was delightful. Preston and I relaxed, watched television, shopped in modern shopping malls, and went swimming at the beach. How I loved being with my mother! Always, we have been close and can spend hours talking about the things of God. How blessed I am to have such a family. My dad usually was working, but when he was home, he joined right in with our discussions. My two sisters would visit and we all had great fun together. Near the end of August, Allen returned to Florida where he and Preston were baptized together at Southside Assembly of God church in Jacksonville. Chet joined us in the States for a short vacation; soon it was time to return to Saudi.

**WADI HANIFA COMPOUND
PRESTON AND FRIENDS COMING HOME FROM SCHOOL**

During the summer while Preston and I were in Florida, Chet moved us into a brand new one hundred family compound in Wadi Hanifa, complete with trees, grass, and a recreation center with swimming pool! Soon we would have tennis courts; Chet and I, avid tennis players, could play every day. Jackie, Homer, and their boys, Chip and Brad, along with Chihuahua Bruce, moved in next door to us. Hurray! It was great to have them for neighbors! Jackie had taken a new position at work and wanted to know if I would be interested in her former job. I said, "Yes!" Within a few days after returning to Saudi, I was working with a contracting company providing restaurant and recreation services for the Corps of Engineers.

My office was located at the Desert Inn, a restaurant and recreation facility for the Corps of Engineers. My job was to keep food supply records and take catering orders for private parties. I worked with a Philippino accountant named Joey who played the guitar and did a great Elvis imitation and a Vietnamese clerk named Jackie who was married to an American engineer. Working with them was never dull! Jackie, who grew up in France and studied pastry making there, often brought us samples of her delicious pastries. Most of her family lived in the States or in Europe. Some of the family remained in Vietnam; it was Jackie's dream to help her Vietnamese relatives get to Europe or the States. The accountant Joey left the Philippines to make money for his family. He was able to go home twice a year to see his wife and two children.

We all got along well; we laughed a lot and still got our work done. Another member of our team who drifted in and out of the office was Leroy. Leroy was not his real name, but my neighbor Jackie named him Leroy, and no one knew any other name for him. Leroy, about nineteen years of age, was a tall, lanky Ethiopian who usually had a grin on his face. I remember that Leroy slept a lot, but always came quickly when we needed him. Leroy was the stock boy who stocked items and counted the merchandise in stock. He called me Taylor, and we got along well. Once, when my driver failed to come take me home, Leroy offered to drive me to the Wadi. Against my better judgment, I agreed to let him drive me. When we got into the car, I knew that I made a mistake. Leroy did not know how to put the key in the ignition! While I showed him about the key and the ignition, he assured me that he was a excellent driver and that I was safe with him! Leroy only had driven stick shift cars; this car had automatic transmission. Soon we were hopping down the road like a rabbit! Leroy was trying to work the gas pedal and the break pedal at the same time. Before we got onto a main road, I gave Leroy a driving lesson and explained what he must do to get me home safely. What a sight it was as I talked and Leroy steered and the car hopped along. When we got to the steep drop in the road leading down into the wadi, Leroy gritted his teeth like he was about to jump off a cliff! I do not think Leroy had ever driven on a hill before; he was convinced that the car would go careening downward. Finally we made it all the way to the wadi and to my front door. Leroy was proud!

In addition to the office staff, I worked with seven versatile, good natured, well educated Egyptian athletes (all men) hired by the Saudis to teach soccer, swimming, and other sports to children of the royal family. Because the Egyptians worked only a few hours a week for the Saudis, there was plenty of time for them to work within our recreation program. Additionally, I worked closely with the cook Akmed who was from Yemen, a country located just south of Saudi Arabia. Akmed had been working for thirty-five years as a cook, mostly for Americans. His English was excellent and he got along well with most people although he could be temperamental. He came into my office daily, and we planned Desert Inn meals and catered menus based on foods we had in stock. It was work that I enjoyed.

Akmed always was in demand for US State Department functions and other private events; part of my job was to help manage his schedule to ensure that there were no overlapping events. He wore a tall white chef's hat with a white apron wrapped around his rather large belly. He was quite professional as he carved the roasts and served the assortment of foods. All of the food was delicious when Akmed was in charge. He could prepare any kind of food, but his specialty was middle eastern foods. I still remember his delicious rolled grape leaves stuffed with rice and meat and spices. He could put together a buffet dinner that was both beautiful and delicious. One of his favorite desserts was honey balls, a little like crisp round doughnut balls coated in honey. He enjoyed mixing with the guests and learning what was happening in Riyadh. Ahmed knew all the gossip! Few secrets were kept from him.

When I look back on these times and working with such great people, I remember how much I thought of each of them. I was privileged to work with so many talented people who came from such diverse backgrounds. They were drawn together by a common bond, each one was aggressive enough to leave family, friends, and country and relocate to a place where they could work and support families who usually remained behind. Each came from a country with severe economic problems, but none of them complained. They were survivors, and each was willing to take the necessary risks associated with working in Saudi Arabia.

One story in particular stands out in my memory. Salah Housney, an Egyptian soccer star, lived in Riyadh with his beautiful wife Nahed and worked with the recreation program. Salah, who was big and strong and jovial, was a favorite of everyone's. Before coming to Riyadh, he won an Egyptian "super bowl" soccer game in Cairo by kicking the winning goal during the final seconds of play. He was carried off the field on the shoulders of his team mates in front of a stadium crowd that had gone wild with winning excitement. One day, while we were working together, he did not come to work. I learned what kept him away. Egypt's courageous President Anwar Sadat had just gone to Israel to make peace overtures to the Israeli government. The success of this brave gesture was heralded around the world as newspapers everywhere carried President Sadat's journey as front page news. The Saudis were furious and for days afterwards were accosting Egyptians in Riyadh and beating them with no mercy. The story told to me about Salah was that it took five large Saudi men to get him to the ground and beat him. I was so sad! Later, I was told that Saudis beating Egyptians in Riyadh is not an unusual occurrence because many Egyptians pride themselves on being "Pharaon" or "from the days of the pharaohs" and do not like being referred to as Arabs. The great Egyptian culture goes back to the most ancient time before Abraham. Egypt has been a unified state for more that five thousand years. Egyptians believe they are a unique people who have given much to world history and culture. Perhaps this is one reason that President Sadat was able to sign a peace agreement with Israel when Arab nations could not acknowledge Israel. In my estimation, Egyptians, by nature, are peace loving people. Their two wars with Israel took the lives of many young men, broke the hearts of many mothers and fathers, and destroyed their economy. I believe President Sadat never wanted another war with Israel. That peace treaty still stands today.

That memorable year ended with a Christmas Party in our new Recreation Center. Many talented people from the Corps family, together with employees and guests from a variety of backgrounds, worked to have a festive, traditional party for the children and a lively get-together for the adults. The program included a reading of the Christmas story, gifts for all the children, games, and great food for everyone. Before eating, we bowed our heads and asked that the great God of the Universe would bless us all

<u>*UNVEILINGS*</u>
<u>*A Desert Journey*</u>
by
Patricia Adora Clark Taylor

CHAPTER EIGHT -- GETTING TO EGYPT
<u>Riyadh, Saudi Arabia -- 1978</u>

CAIRO, MAY 1978 – Me on a Camel with Egyptian Friends

In January of 1978, a decision was made to enlarge the recreation program, and I left the food services branch to work full time in the recreation branch as the Community Coordinator. 1978 was the year I planned numerous recreation events for Corps families in Riyadh. It also was the year I went to Cairo with an Egyptian friend to visit with her family. (The photo above was made during my Cairo visit; it was a real highlight of that year.)

The Corps of Engineers was opening two new recreation centers for three hundred families. Planned activities of real interest to the Corps community was crucial for success. Together with another American woman, I designed a recreation program by combining the skill of the Egyptian athletes with the unique talents of others in Riyadh. Soon we were joined by a third American woman, a skilled arts and crafts specialist. The three of us recruited talent from within the Corps community. I was amazed at the variety of skills. Soon, I met with nine women, talented and eager to begin projects that they enjoyed while teaching others. The problem we faced throughout the program was getting teaching and craft materials into the country because of an endless mountain of paper work for government officials (both US and Saudi) that kept us going in circles.

Nevertheless, we accomplished much in a relatively short time. Our goal was to get a variety of recreation classes started as soon as possible and to have an outstanding, well organized summer program with something of interest for everyone. The classes that emerged from that first meeting were Conversational French, Sewing Lessons, Macramé, Arabic Culture and Cooking, China Painting, and Chinese Cooking. Soon we added Children's Drama, Comparative Study of Christianity and Islam, Beginner's Bridge, Indoor Gardening, Karate, Modern Dance, Belly Dancing, First Aid, Classical Music Appreciation, and an informative International Lecture Series on a variety of subjects.

**ME LEADING A "RECREATION TOUR"
OF RIYADH UNIVERSITY CONSTRUCTION SITE**

Always, there were hurdles to overcome! Excellent communication was necessary to ensure successful planning and implementation. Before any event, everything had to be spelled out specifically, and responsibilities had to be clearly defined. If we were having an event with food, there could be no last minute confusion about who managed refrigeration, who transported food and party items, who transported personnel, who did the clean up, who paid the bills. If we used school buses to transport party goers (as we often did), we had to ensure that our drivers were on time and drove safely. We never wanted to have a mix up with our Arab drivers, so we continually worked on maintaining good relations and good communication.

RIYADH UNIVERSITY CONSTRUCTION --
OUR TOUR GROUP LEARNED OF THE PLANNING
FOR A HUGE UNIVERSITY

Chet and I teamed up to manage one particularly important event. He was the event coordinator for the Corps and I was the event coordinator for the contractor. We worked well together and the three day event (May 12 to May 15) went as smooth as glass -- well, almost. The event brought Corps of Engineers couples from all over Saudi Arabia to Riyadh for a Corps of Engineer conference that included well-planned luncheons, dinners, and organized touring and shopping time. Some Corps couples lived at extremely remote sites and were delighted to have time away in the big city! The first day "meet and greet" affair was a picnic and bar-b-que at the residence of the Corps of Engineer's general in charge of the Saudi work. The next morning after breakfast, the men went into business meetings. The women boarded buses and went to the Museum of Antiquities for an interesting tour. Ancient artifacts on display were from locations throughout Saudi Arabia, giving a description of Saudi Arabia's unique history. Afterwards, there was shopping at the suqs and lunch at the Desert Inn. That evening's event was in the Wadi Hanifa compound where the recreation rooms and lighted outdoor pool and patio areas were transformed by real flowers, date palm fronds, candles, Hawaiian music (interspersed with Arabic music), and tables filled with wonderful food. The Wadi Hanifa Luau was in full swing as Chet and I relaxed outside at a table by the pool. People were dancing, talking, eating, and having a great time. Nahed, Salah's wife, taught belly dancing classes and some of her students performed that night with gusto! A good time was had by all. Chet and I were happy that our efforts were successful, even though we still had challenges ahead! The next day there was a full schedule beginning with breakfast, followed by morning activities, then lunch at the Riyadh Intercontinental Hotel's dining room, followed by a tour of the city. That evening buses were provided to take guests to the Riyadh Water Tower Restaurant, located at the top of the water tower high above the city, for a formal dinner catered by the Desert Inn. Crystal, china, and silverware were placed with precision on each table.

The dining event that evening went without a hitch -- almost. With me that evening were seven young women, sixteen to eighteen years of age, who were daughters of Corps personnel. They were lovely in long dresses and enjoyed assisting me with the evening. For them, I think it was fun to do something different in Riyadh, to see the city at night from the water tower, and to get paid for an evening's work. The event was over at ten p.m. Suddenly I realized that everyone had gone except me and two of the young women who stayed with me. We made one last look through the restaurant to ensure that it was left clean and in order. Our driver was waiting below; we stepped into the elevator, pushed the button, and started down to the ground floor exit. Suddenly, the elevator stopped and would go no further. Frantically, I began pushing buttons. Nothing happened. I called on the intercom to the guard below. He spoke no English and did not understand my Arabic. It was a frightening moment for the three of us, but I remained calm. I knew the girls were terrified. After a few minutes, another elevator came down beside us and the side door to our elevator opened; we were looking directly into the opened side door of the other elevator; several grinning Saudi faces came into view. (As I learned later, this was not an unusual occurrence and they were used to rescuing frightened passengers.) The Saudis motioned to us. All we had to do was follow the one Saudi who had opened the side door of our elevator and walk across a cross beam from one elevator to the other elevator. As I removed my high heel shoes, I told the girls that if I could do it, they certainly could do it. I stepped out onto the beam which crossed the dark chasm between the two elevators. Below me was a dark pit that went down, down, down. I crossed carefully and quickly; then stepped into the working elevator. One by one, the girls followed me to safety. The Saudi guards congratulated us, and we congratulated one another. What an end to an otherwise perfect day! I never again saw that tower without remembering the elevator experience.

The next day the guests departed, and I took a week's vacation. I now was thirty-six years old. I first left the States when I was twenty-seven years old to be with Chet on Okinawa. Since then we moved every couple of years from Okinawa where Preston was born to Kwajalein to Hawaii to Maryland to Italy to Saudi Arabia. In Riyadh, I had been working long hours since the past September when I first began work for the contractor. I hardly knew who I was anymore. There were times when I wanted to stop, to get off the merry-go-round, but I did not know how to stop the music. Nahed was going home to Cairo for two weeks to visit her family, and she invited me to come with her to visit for a week. Chet, Salah, Nahed, and I had become good friends; Salah insisted that I would be safe with Nahed's family. (Salah recovered from the beating which hospitalized him for several days.) Nahed was a lovely woman in her twenties; she was very much in love with her husband. The two of them grew up in the same neighborhood in Cairo where they lived across the street from one another. They were some of my favorite people. I knew I was fortunate to have been invited to stay for a week with Nahed's family.

Preston, now a fifth grader, was happy in the new compound with the recreation activities, with his friends, and with his schoolwork. His international school was more advanced than American schools, and he was busy researching and writing essays and studying math. Everyone was doing well; it was a good time to get away. Within a few days, Nahed and I flew from Riyadh to Cairo. During the flight, we had a conversation about our families. Nahed wanted to know about my family in the States; I wanted to know about her family in Cairo. As we spoke, I realized two things that surprised me. The first was that most of Nahed's family had never met an American. The second was that Nahed's father was one of President Sadat's important generals; he and the President were close friends. Nahed warned me that when the plane landed in Cairo, we would be escorted away from the plane by her father, and then whisked through customs into the waiting arms of her large family. I braced myself for the meetings ahead. Suddenly, I felt that I was representing America!

The plane landed in Cairo and came to a stop. Steps were put into place for everyone to disembark. Sure enough, there was Nahed's father in his uniform. When Nahed got to the bottom of the steps, her father hugged her and welcomed her home! Nahed introduced us and we shook hands. We walked through customs into the airport waiting area where about twenty of Nahed's family and friends were waving their hands at us and shouting and laughing and crying. Suddenly, we were in the middle of everyone, and Nahed was introducing me while everyone was talking. I did not know any of the family; but I was a friend of Nahed's, and that was enough for them to embrace me as family! The crowd moved toward a curb outside where I would see the Cairo traffic whizzing by us. Nahed and I got into a very small black European car, then about seven other people, all friends and family, crammed inside. Then we were flying through the Cairo traffic with the windows down and with our passengers as much outside the car as they were inside. There was laughter, singing, and clapping of hands. Throughout my stay in Cairo, there was a rhythm to everything we did. Handclapping, while singing or talking, could break out at any time; it was a common form of expression. At first it was unnerving; but during the drive, I joined the rhythm.

We drove toward the apartment of Nahed's sister Nadia and Nadia's husband Asmy. Asmy was serving time in the army in a tank battalion; Nadia was a student at Cairo University where she studied to be a pharmacist. As we drove along, everyone was talking at once and asking questions about Saudi Arabia. I was surprised to learn that they found the old customs and ways of Saudi as unbelievable as I found them. These Egyptians were modern! About twenty minutes from the airport, we arrived in a nice section of town with a number of modern, more expensive looking, multistory apartments. Each apartment had a balcony. Nadia's apartment building was all white with lots of balconies and windows, and it had no elevator. We walked up six flights of stairs to get to Nadia's apartment. (No comment was made about the stairs; walking up stairs was great exercise and a real energy saver!) We could tell that Nadia was bursting with excitement to show off her new apartment. She and Asmy had not been married for long and only recently acquired the apartment. When we went inside, I was surprised to see beautiful furnishings in a French provincial style. I thought, "How can this be?" I asked where the furniture was made and was surprised to learn that it was made in Egypt, as were the lovely carpets and the exquisite light fixtures. I had no idea that the Egyptians were such craftsmen. No wonder so many of them worked in Italy! Many of the Egyptians spoke Italian and had lived in Italy. Between my Italian and my conversational Arabic and my English, I was able to communicate with everyone.

When the others left, we had hot tea, and relaxed together. Nadia showed Nahed and me to our room which opened onto a small balcony where we would have breakfast in the morning. The weather was absolutely perfect, and I breathed a sigh of relief as I realized that I was going to have an enjoyable time with lovely, hospitable people. I was impressed with the preparation Nadia made for our visit. Our bedroom was spotless, as was the rest of the apartment, and everything was in order. Much care had gone into the furnishing of this apartment; it was obvious that Nadia was a person who paid attention to detail. She showed me her modern clothes, that were beautifully designed, cut, and sewn by Nadia herself. She was a fashion expert and wanted to show me the local shops with their stylish Egyptian cotton dresses. We got back into our little car and headed for a shopping district where I had great fun trying on stylish shoes and dresses. With the help of Nadia and Nahed, I selected two cotton dresses for day and two lovely dresses for evening.

After my purchases, we went to see Samir the hairdresser who took one look at me and knew just how to cut my hair around my face so that it would flip back and look more modern. At first I was frightened to have Samir work on my hair. Placed next to Samir's styling chair was a tray of red hot coals with a curling iron in the midst of the coals. No electricity was used for such styling. I watched as Nahed's hair was being styled and saw the steam come off her jet black hair. I was sure that curling iron would burn the hair off my head! Samir stilled my fears. When he was finished with Nahed, she looked even more beautiful. I sat in the chair; once he began working with my hair, I was totally at ease. He, too, was a craftsman. When he was finished cutting, washing, and styling my hair, I loved it!

We returned to Nadia's apartment for tea and Egyptian cakes on the balcony. It was a perfect spring afternoon. I was exhausted, so I got undressed and went to bed for several hours. Suddenly, I awoke refreshed and excited about the evening. It was ten p.m., and I put on one of my new dresses. We were about to experience Cairo's Egyptian nightlife. We drove to an older hotel-nightclub where we met about twenty other family members; some were young, and some were grandparents. There was much hugging as everyone continued to welcome Nahed home. Immediately hearty appetizers, which were a meal in themselves, were placed on our tables. The band was terrific and could play anything from Latin sambas to waltzes to Arabic dances to rock and roll. We all danced and danced and had a great time! The featured singer sang a beautiful ballad about a young Egyptian, caught in the "Six Days War" with Israel, who wanted only to live in peace and return to his beloved land of Egypt. The song came out of the war and became a theme song for Egyptians. After the song, he asked me to stand up. I did so; all around me were Egyptians in the crowded nightclub. The spotlight was on me. He introduced me to the crowd and then dedicated the song to me and to all Americans. Everyone clapped in agreement. It was an overwhelming experience, and I was delighted to be so warmly welcomed to Egypt by Egyptians. So many Americans travel as tourists to Egypt; but here I was in an Egyptian nightclub not frequented by Americans. I was among Egyptians who rarely would have an opportunity to meet an American. The entire week I was in Egypt I was a celebrity because I was an American. People wanted to see me, to hear me, to interact with me. Just as Nahed told me on the airplane, most of them never had met an American.

CAIRO NIGHTCLUB WITH EGYPTIAN FRIENDS

The second day of my visit began as I sat on Nadia's balcony in the warm Egyptian sun with Nadia and Nahed. Nahed's mother came over to have breakfast with us. She also was a beautiful, regal Egyptian woman. She brought us delicious pastries and creamy white cheese. She hugged Nahed and wanted to know all about the previous night. We told her all about the evening; she was so happy to know that we were enjoying ourselves! It was obvious to me that Nahed's family had been worried about Nahed living in Saudi. It was apparent to me that the Egyptians were not terribly fond of the

Saudis. As we were conversing together in English and Arabic, Nadia brought out Arabic flat bread, more cheese, olives, hard boiled eggs, and lots of hot tea. I was completely relaxed; the food tasted good in the morning air. Most of the conversation was in Arabic with me understanding, generally, what was going on, thanks in part to Nahed's quick translations. Nahed, Nadia, and their mother enjoyed one another's company and reminisced about old times. We spent the rest of the morning relaxing, talking, and just being happy. I was so happy. I was happy that Chet and I made the decision to move to Saudi Arabia; I was happy that I met so many outstanding people in the desert; I was happy to have a friend like Nahed; I was happy to be in this place with these people at this time in my life. Decades of my life would come and would go and still I would remember the bright Egyptian morning, the friendly faces, and the love I felt for these individuals.

We dressed at noon, by one p.m. we were in the shops. Then we drove to the pyramids and had lemonade, afterwards I road a camel in the desert near the pyramids and had my picture taken. It was a lovely day. About four p.m. we drove to a restaurant beside a lovely man-made lake surrounded by a walkway where families walked with their children. The lake and the walkway were surrounded by green weeping willow trees that seemed to bow down towards the blue lake. Ducks were swimming in the lake; and everywhere I looked, I saw beautiful flowers. We had lunch on the terrace by the lake. Lunch consisted of fresh tomatoes, squash, cucumbers, onions, Arabic bread, Arabic dip, and baked chicken. It was a perfect meal for the afternoon! I could write on and on about that week! That night we drove to Alexandria to spend two days at the beach with more of Nahed's family who were not so well off. Here several family members lived together in sparsely furnished apartments just across the street from the sea. It made no difference to me about the look of their home because the hospitality was always the same. Nahed's cousins were so good to us. I learned that the responsibilities of educated members of a family are many. They educate other members of the family and help with the cost of housing which is very expensive. Everyone cares for each other and children are treated with a great deal of love. Children are the bright spot in the lives of the Egyptians, and people are happy with the simple things in life. The Egyptians gain strength from their families and there is a joy that shines through their problems. Never did we get into a car that someone did not break out into a chanting song accompanied by hands clapping to the rhythm.

WITH FRIENDS AT THE BEACH IN ALEXANDRIA, EGYPT

One of Nahed's cousins in his thirties was an accountant and had just graduated from college. Still unmarried, he supported his sisters and his mother, and was putting his brother through college. He had worked hard for a number of years just to get through college. Tall, broad-shoulder, polite, well-mannered, and handsome, he was one of the most exquisite men I have ever met. That night we danced by the sea. I relaxed in his arms. The attraction was strong, and I remember how good it felt to be so close to him. I knew my responsibility was to return to Saudi and to Chet, Preston, and all the family that I loved. Still, we had a wonderful time; and still I remember him. Even now, I hope he is alive and well. We swam in the sea and danced in an old palace by the sea that once belonged to King Farouk, who was displaced when Egypt became a republic in 1953. We sat on the beach cross-legged and ate fresh seafood roasted over the outdoor fire. In the background there was only the sound of Egyptian music and ocean waves crashing to the shore.

Twenty-five years later, I still hear the sound of waves crashing in the background and feel the soft Egyptian sea air as we spoke of the way things are in the world. There was happiness in the voices of the Egyptians that night; but they were sad about the great loss of Egyptian lives in the war and desperately wanted to have the Egyptian Sinai returned to Egypt by the Israelis. The Six Days War left them hoping for better times but fearful that things may not turn out as hoped for; I knew they wanted peace. Several times that night they asked me why Americans are willing to arm Israel as it does; they seemed genuinely perplexed by this. I had no real answer. My prayer that night and even now is that God blesses the Egyptians with great prosperity and lasting peace.

The entire week was lovely. I had a wonderful visit with Nahed's parents at their very nice apartment. Theirs was an older apartment building in Cairo. The elevator was the kind with the rod iron accordion door that closed across the elevator opening. Nahed and I went to the third floor. We entered their beautifully furnished apartment; once more I met the General. He spoke in Arabic, then told me in English that he was surprised how well I understood his Arabic. I was pleased with his compliment. It was interesting to me that many of the older Egyptians spoke English because, as children, they learned it in public school. The General told me in recent years there is a growing pride in Egyptian culture, so English is not taught as it once was in public school. We spoke briefly of the war. Everywhere I went I heard about the number of Egyptian sons lost in tanks in the desert in the war. Egypt was still in a time of grief. When I heard the Egyptians speak of the war, I knew they never wanted it to happen again; and I realized that President Sadat was under a lot of pressure to regain the land that was lost to Israel.

THE EGYPTIANS IN CAIRO – ASMY, NADIA, AND NAHED

When we returned to Nadia's apartment, there was much excitement because "Auntie" was visiting from Sudan. Nahed hugged her Auntie and was so happy to see her. One scene stands out in my memory of that afternoon. Auntie was in the bedroom sitting in front of a dresser with a tall three way mirror attached to it. Nahed was standing behind her and combing Auntie's long black hair. I walked up behind Nahed. All three of us were reflected in the mirror. Suddenly, Nahed took Auntie's black face in her hands and said to me, "See how beautiful she is; look at her perfect face." I looked into a firm black face without a wrinkle, with high cheekbones, and with the most incredibly gorgeous almond shaped eyes. She smiled at me and I saw it -- behind the jet black skin were all the colors of the rainbow that came together like a delicate watercolor painting. The colors radiated through the soft moistness of the skin. There we were, the three of us. I was Caucasian with olive skin; Nahed was Egyptian brown, and Auntie was Sudanese black. We were a painting in need of a painter. I wish I could recapture that moment. Nahed wanted me to stay another week and go with her and Auntie to visit Sudan, but I declined the invitation knowing that I must return to Riyadh. Auntie spoke in Arabic and Nahed translated. "I will carry you on my head," was her gentle way of letting us know that she would take great care of us. It was an endearing expression.

I wish I could have gone to Sudan. Nahed described it as a beautiful country even though it was impoverished. Later I read in a newspaper that Sudan could not even make its

United Nations dues. It made me sad; I remembered that Nahed and her family are of Sudanese ancestry and how they spoke with pleasure of their trips to Sudan to visit relatives.

(Note: President Sadat, working with President Jimmy Carter and Israel's President Begin, made a huge difference in the Middle East by working through negotiations to bring about a desired outcome for Egypt. I could not have known it in May of 1978 when I was in Cairo, but four years later, in May 1982, Israel would return the Sinai to Egypt. At that time, Chet and I would be living in Israel as a part a peace keeping mission to help bring about the return of the Sinai!)

UNVEILINGS
A Desert Journey
by
Patricia Adora Clark Taylor

CHAPTER NINE -- OVERCOMING HURDLES
Riyadh, Saudi Arabia -- 1978

1978 Me in Backyard – B-2 Compound – Wadi Hanifa

My work was waiting for me when I returned to Riyadh in May. The general in charge of the US Army Corps of Engineers work in Saudi Arabia was leaving Riyadh for another assignment. His farewell party was to be a traditional desert "goat grab" for three hundred people. A "goat grab" is a Bedouin meal of roasted goat served on a huge platter and surrounded by white rice. Huge round stainless steel trays are needed for the stuffed and cooked goat carcass, which is placed in the center of the tray with rice all around! Traditionally, it is served in a desert setting in a spacious Bedouin tent where Bedouin sit cross-legged in a circle on large carpets as trays are passed from one person to another. Each person uses his right hand to scoop up a hand full of rice and then takes a portion of meat. For the general's farewell event, we planned on twenty stuffed goats, fifty bar-b-qued chickens, tabouli (chopped parsley salad), rolled grape leaves, relish trays, and traditional Saudi tea. The Saudi National Guard donated large tents, along with the traditional, durable Saudi carpets make of course wool to go on the ground inside the tents. The big, spacious Bedouin tents were erected in such a way that three hundred people could sit comfortably in circular groups of about twenty each.

Organization of this event was a major feat. It was necessary that everything be planned precisely and then carried out as planned. People in much higher positions than mine decided the Desert Inn would not prepare the entire meal as planned; instead, the Saudi National Guard would prepare and cook the goats. I did not think this was a good idea, but the decision was made and would not be reversed. That night the evening went well, the food was delicious, and the next day eighty people were sick, including the general. Fortunately, they all recovered from their nausea and fortunately Chet and I and friends did not get sick.

In June, Allen arrived and was happy to be home. It was good to have him in the house, and he and Preston were happy to be together again. The two of them have remained close, even with the separations. Allen's goal was to work again this summer to buy camera equipment. As for my work, the recreation summer program was imminent; unfortunately, the plans we made in January for the summer program had not been carried out by management. Necessary materials had not been ordered, and there was no final program agenda. Somewhere within management there was a decision making problem about implementation of the program. The summer arrived on time with 120 degree heat, teenagers arrived home from school abroad, and unsupervised children on summer vacation from the Riyadh International School were loose in the compounds! Most of the mothers now were working with the American government or with contractors because anyone with office skills was in demand and the pay was very good. In a frantic and overdue response, management devised an overkill disorganized program that wasted time and money. Instead of using versatile Egyptians and others on staff in a productive manner, there was a quick decision to bring college students from the States and pay them to help run the summer program. Untold amounts of money were spent recruiting college athletes from the States. Soon, these young adults arrived from the States and were in my office demanding to know what they were supposed to do, where they were supposed to go, and why there was disorganization. Unfortunately, many of them lacked both the people skills and the maturity of our regular staff. In fact our Stateside "summer directors" knew nothing about Middle East or Saudi history or culture and were, themselves, in need of supervision; and with additional personnel, we needed more vehicles and drivers. There was no money available for either, so our summer personnel, who flew from the States to Riyadh, often could not get from their compounds to work locations.

Soon July 4th arrived and was celebrated with three different parties at three different Corps compound locations for a total of five hundred guests. All the parties were supported by the contractor; I was the event coordinator. Our detailed planning led to well-coordinated events. I traveled from one location to another, using the short-wave radio to call for additional help or more tables, chairs, and tablecloths. The parties were successful, and I was tired but happy.

While working through the problems of party planning and summer personnel, I was given two weeks notice to plan and implement sightseeing tours around Riyadh for Corps personnel and families. This meant scheduling buses and drivers and getting approval from various officials. I spent a week with my driver going, in person, from place to place in the summer heat to get immediate approval from US and Saudi officials for Americans to visit particular Riyadh locations and be allowed to take photographs. At the same time, I was coordinating with Yemen drivers and with management to get buses assigned to me on certain days. The vehicles, which were new when I arrived in Saudi, now were breaking down daily and were in need of constant repair because they had been driven non-stop over rough desert terrain. Also, my drivers were always hiding away during the day and sleeping, not because they were lazy, but because they were smart. Only Americans are foolish enough to keep working non-stop in 120 degree heat; even southern Europeans know enough about climate to rest in the afternoon.

I began working on the tour project. The tours were important because they provided a unique opportunity for Corps families to have personal interaction with Saudi Arabia's places and people. As part of the tour preparation, I went with my driver to visit two interesting Saudi sites and I met with officials at the sites who actually were excited about having American visitors from the Corps community. One location was the new Riyadh University, still under construction, and another site was the new Riyadh Sports City. After checking out the site personally, I gave my drivers their driving directions ahead of time, because it was useless for me, a woman, to give a Saudi or Yemen driver orders in front of others. On the day of the tour, the "tourists" met me at my office where they boarded buses. As we were riding along, I sat in a front seat, spoke about different areas of the city's history, and answered questions until we reached the site. Once at the tour site, a knowledgeable guide would walk us through the location and give pertinent information. Then there was opportunity for photographs. My feedback from the people on the Riyadh tours was, "Keep those tours coming!" The reasons for their popularity were because men and women could get outside the boundaries of their everyday lives, see places that they might never have known about otherwise, and get unique photos or movies for private collections. If our passengers tried to get these photos and movies on their own, it could be more difficult due to Saudi customs and rules. Even now, Preston remembers not being allowed to photograph the gold suqs which fascinated him when he was only a child living in Saudi.

In July, I planned two Riyadh photographic tours of the city, one for children and one for adults. One of my drivers and I toured the city and mapped out a tour plan with plenty of historic sites and interesting areas. The day of the children's tour, July 19th, I had a bus filled with excited children with cameras and a few parents for chaperones. Each child received a copy of the tour map. As we were driving along, they took photos while I spoke with them. I was pleased they showed such interest. We stopped at some of the sites and let them get out to take more photos. We ended the afternoon with refreshments at one of the recreation centers. The children enjoyed the tour, and I was happy with their reaction. The next day, July 20th, was the adult tour. I was looking forward to the day because the previous day had gone so well. The adult response for this tour was impressive; today, instead of one bus, there would be three buses filled with a total of one hundred and twenty-five tour passengers.

I arrived at work and saw two of my drivers who knew the route; but my lead driver, who was with me yesterday, was absent. The only driver available to take his place was an unpleasant one who was not my favorite person because he was not a "team player." Nevertheless, the passengers arrived and filled the three buses. Each one received a tour map, along with information about Riyadh and its history. I stepped into the lead bus with the unpleasant driver. We began the tour route, and I was feeling very much in charge! Suddenly, the driver swerved the bus down another street and began speaking in Arabic. It appeared that he decided to be the tour guide. I was furious and commanded him to turn around and get back to the planned route. Following behind us were the two other buses with their bewildered drivers.

Finally, all three buses stopped in the middle of a suq area and my bus driver opened the hood of our bus saying that something was wrong with the bus. Saudi people gathered around us. A man came walking through the crowd with a herd of goats. All three bus drivers climbed on top of the bus and began poking the engine. The amazing part of this fiasco was that the bus passengers could have cared less about my plans. They were photographing and making movies of me arguing with the bus driver, of the bus drivers on top of the bus, of the man with the goats, of the people standing around. It was a regular movie, and they were delighted to capture such vivid action shots. It all ended as quickly as it began. My ridiculous driver got back in the bus; the other drivers got back in their buses, and the happy passengers, having shot rolls of film, got back in their seats. My driver returned to the regular route and the rest of the day went without a hitch; but, looking back, I believe the best part of the day for the passengers was the unplanned side trip into the suq. That afternoon, when the tour ended, the passengers came up to me, one by one, and congratulated me for having such an outstanding tour!

Daily life at the compound was improving; but at home, Chet was more exhausted than I was due to his own problems at work. Fifteen year old Allen was encountering a few problems. His job was to supervise a Yemen furniture moving crew and to keep the crew from tossing furniture out of second story windows because it was easier than carrying furniture down the stairs. The crew, in turn, tried to convert Allen to Islam. The conversion did not take, but they did convince him to buy a prayer rug and pray in the direction of Mecca. This interest ended when Allen arrived back at school in the States and his housemother put the rug in the washing machine. Allen returned to his room after classes and saw large puff balls on his bed, remnants of a prayer rug!

Only Preston and his friends were having a truly great time because the recreation center was open with its long summer hours, its big swimming pool, and numerous programs. One successful program was a ping pong tournament in which ping pong champions from the Korean and Philippine communities were invited to participate with the Corps community. Championship ping pong became a great spectator sport, really exciting to watch! Children and adults began to try out for a spot on the Corps "ping pong team." Surprise, Preston became one of the champions who went into the finals! He played well against the adult foreign workers and was defeated only at the very end of the tournament. We congratulated him for being a real ping pong champion! In the compound, our dog Julie, also, was doing very well. She was allowed outside, within the compound walls, if supervised by Allen or Preston. She make friends with our neighbors and their animals. One of our neighbors had a feisty cat. Julie charged the cat a couple of times; the cat responded with claws. Within a few days Julie and the cat were friends and would sit quietly together on my neighbor's porch. Once some of the boys in the compound, playing kickball in front of our house, accidentally kicked the ball into our large front window and cracked it. Such incidents were typical of daily compound life; but, in general, life in our compound was without serious trouble.

Family Fishing Trips – Even in Saudi Arabia

One day, one of the drivers put a large cardboard box on my desk at work. Inside was a fat desert lizard about four feet long from its head to the end of its very long tail. It was covered with ugly lizard scales; only its mother could love such an animal! It was known as a "daub" or desert lizard. It was dangerous only as long as it could manipulate its long scaly, spiny tail in such a way as to inflict injury to its enemy. The bus driver made a pet out of the lizard by breaking its tail which rendered it harmless. He had a string tied around its neck so he could walk his lizard. He no longer wanted the pet and thought I might like to have it. I did; I thought it would be an unusual pet for Preston who was fond of all kinds of animals. I took the lizard home with me in the box and put it in the backyard. The lizard showed no signs of trying to get out of the box. Preston came home and saw it and was amazed to be looking at a huge lizard in our backyard. He didn't say much. The next day as always, the pool at the recreation center was filled with our compound's children who were laughing and playing. Suddenly a huge lizard leaped into the middle of the pool with the children and was happily swimming around. I'll bet that lizard had never seen that much water! In an instant the children were out of that pool. Preston said he had never seen kids scramble that fast! Everyone wanted to know where the lizard came from, but Preston didn't say a word. After a short time, the lizard hopped out of the pool and ran away. The lizard has never been seen again.

On a few occasions, veiled Saudi women who lived in a nearby village, would walk down the dusty road from their home and wander through our compound with their children. It was as much a novelty for us as it was for them. I think we all enjoyed those visits from our Saudi neighbors. Each day as I left my house to go to work, I passed their small Saudi village which consisted of a few square shaped clay huts with flat roofs and wood doors. There were small pens for goats, but mostly the goats ran free with the barefooted children on the hardened Saudi desert clay. The children, who were slim and brown-skinned with dark eyes and wavy hair, always smiled and waved and ran after us when we passed by in our cars. Beyond the village, we crossed the river bed and went up, up, and up along a paved road which took us out of the river bed past the splendid palace of Prince Fahd. Nearby, down in the wadi, was wealthy Prince Bandar's farm. I could only imagine that our Saudi neighbors must have been their poor relatives. After passing Prince Fahd's palace, we had a short ride to connect with one of the main roads going into Riyadh. For a year and a half, I made that trip almost every day. The memories still remain of dirt roads, dusty highways with heat emanating from black pavement, laughing children playing in the dirt, and elegant palaces.

Once, while living in Saudi but vacationing in the States, I had a dream of two palaces. The scene was set in Saudi Arabia in a wadi area. On a hill overlooking the wadi was a beautiful palace. I was familiar with this palace which belonged to Prince Fahd, heir to the throne of Saudi Arabia. Then my attention was directed down into the river bed and followed the winding river bed for about a mile east until I could see another large structure under construction down among the lush greenery of date palms. As I followed this view of the wadi, I heard a voice clearly saying, "This is the summer palace (referring to Prince Fahd's palace) and this is the winter palace (referring to the palace under construction.) When the winter palace is complete, destruction will come." That was the end of the dream. It was August 1978, and I awoke from the dream wondering about it. In September 1978, Chet and I returned to Saudi and drove in the river bed past the little village, but instead of going up towards main roads, we kept driving along the river bed towards a place that we had been told was Prince Bandar's farm. When we reached the farm we peeked through the trees and saw a large structure under construction. I did not know the meaning of the dream or even if there was a meaning, but I was surprised to see construction as was in the dream. Later, I heard rumors that Prince Fahd and Prince Bandar represented opposing views of the Saudi monarchy. I wondered if Prince Fahd and Prince Bandar each were building their own "houses" or political power structures.

UNVEILINGS
A Desert Journey
by
Patricia Adora Clark Taylor

CHAPTER TEN -- SOUTHERN ROOTS
Riyadh, Saudi Arabic -- 1978

1978 Riyadh – Nahed and I Belly Dancing in My Living Room with Linda Henry and Friends

In August we all went back to the States for visits in Florida and Tennessee. We had completed two years in Saudi Arabia, but we decided to extend for six more months. This would give us time to wait for a Maryland job to come available for Chet, allowing us to return to our Maryland home. So we went to the States knowing that all of us, except Allen, would return to Saudi for a time. We looked forward to the day we would return to our Maryland home and life on the Magothy River. Allen, especially, was looking forward to that day.

In August, we landed in Jacksonville, Florida, and it was good to be see our families! I returned to church services at Southside Assembly of God Church. It was wonderful to hear the large choir sing hymns and praises to God. Everything was green and beautiful;

even the people were beautiful! It was hard to believe that planet Earth could have places as vastly different as Florida and Saudi Arabia. We had traveled from a place, half way around the world, where a cross is forbidden. Even in Chet's Saudi construction, a particular part of a structure might be torn down if it resembled the shape of a cross. Yet, here I was in a beautiful church that was open to anyone. The carpet was plush, the musical instruments were well-tuned, and the pastor spoke to men, women, and children in the same congregation about a God who loved them and sent his son to die and be raised up again so the human race could spend eternity with the great God of the universe. The overriding law for each of us was to love God with all our heart and to love our neighbors as ourselves. No motawa with his long stick would come in and arrest us for being open and brazen Christians! It was my hope, having come from a part of the world that represented about a billion Moslems, that America would never lose such freedom.

During the month of August, we traveled from Florida to Elizabethton, Tennessee for a family reunion with Chet's mother's family and to visit Chet's father's relatives. His father was killed in World War II, and the gravesite was high on a Tennessee hill in a beautiful location. We enjoyed vacationing with family, especially Chet's mother, stepfather, and his two sisters with their families. Chet's grandmother, Granny Holsclaw, was living and so were her twelve children, many grandchildren, and a few great-grandchildren. Many people came together to celebrate Granny Holsclaw's birthday, and I remember the wonderful food which was prepared by friends and relatives. It was wonderful to see friendly women all around me who were not covered in black gauze and whose faces shone brightly in the hot August sun! All of us, men and women, mixed together and there was no motawa to come and beat us with a stick! There was a slide presentation of "Granny, This is Your Life" which featured photos from Granny's past, along with popular music depicting the time of the photo. All of us, including the children, were thoroughly entertained; and we appreciated the effort required for such a production!

From the time Chet and I met as teenagers, I have enjoyed traveling to Tennessee to visit with his mother's family. Granny Holsclaw is one of my favorite people. When she was a child, she crossed the mountains with her family in a covered wagon to relocate from North Carolina to Tennessee. She and Grandpa Holsclaw, who died a few years earlier, raised their twelve children by Christian principles. The family, poor in material things, showed great hospitality and always shared what they had with others. Chet's mother has these qualities, as does Chet; he and I enjoy entertaining around the world with friends. I can see how God guided me in selecting a marriage partner. The strong, solid things of God were intertwined within this family and were inherent in Chet who was far more mature that most young men his age. How much I loved him then and how much I still do! When I think of how God has richly blessed us with this marriage and how we take God's mightiest miracles for granted, it leaves me in awe of a God who continues to love us through all of life's peaks and valleys. For Allen especially, this family has meant so very much during his separation from us. When Allen cannot be with us for holidays, he sometimes visits with relatives in Tennessee. Both of our children love Tennessee with its soaring green mountains stretching down into valleys with crystal clear streams flowing over shinning rocks and pebbles; it is God's country!

What a transition! From Saudi Arabia to Tennessee, opposite ends of the earth! I wondered why my life was such a patchwork of people and places. What meaning was there in hopping back and forth from ancient to modern and back to ancient again? What purpose was there in six more months of Saudi Arabia ? Why did I have to return to heat and dust and brown color and crazy traffic and pitiful people and flies and deranged religious systems and smothering living conditions and insanity everywhere? Somewhere there should be a psychiatrist to declare the entire country insane and build an asylum for Saudis before they come spilling out to endanger the rest of the world!

In September I again turned my face to Saudi Arabia hoping it would be my last trip back into the barren desert. I returned to work where things were going smoother since summer was over and children were in school. I was happy to return to Christian friends in my compound. I was meeting once a week in homes for Bible study and fellowship. I did not understand it then, but the great God of the universe was preparing me for all the years ahead of me. I was beginning to feel tired all the time. All the previous years of traveling, adjusting, and living in military environments was beginning to get to me in ways that I did not understand. Saudi Arabia, especially, was difficult. The previous year of working in a job with so much pressure in a hostile environment, plus international travel, was wearing me down.

On Fridays, our Christian services led by Dr. Woodberry, were growing. The choir had become a beautiful expression of praise and love for God; it was a tremendous blessing for all who attended. More and more, Dr. Woodberry was trying to give us Christ-love for Saudi Arabia and its people. I knew it must hurt him to see so many Christians on the endless treadmill of making more and more money. He was the one who was called at all hours to council with wayward children or with husbands and wives trying to deal with the environment, families, jobs, and with one another. Dr. Woodberry certainly was God's man for the hour. Never have I met a more compassionate person. He was familiar with all the problems of the Middle East including problems associated with illegal drugs which were easily available in Saudi Arabia. We heard stories of young adults working in Saudi who could get drugs and, without being caught, bring them into American compounds. I began to realize the enormity of the drug problem.

In such a hostile environment, Christians banded together. We planned picnics in the desert on Friday afternoons so that families could get together and children could run and play together. These events always were successful, especially for people isolated in single houses. The Christian women's group that met once a week continued to grow and was about to outgrow a single house. Every day as I went to work, I passed Riyadh Sports City, the huge sports complex near our compound. I prayed that one day Christian men, women, and children from all parts of the world would meet together to sing out praises to the great God of the universe without reprisal. I knew it was an impossible dream; nevertheless I continued to pray.

Most of all, I prayed that the women of Saudi Arabia, modern day slaves, would be freed from their bondage. When I was a teenager in Florida, I was elected Governor of Girls States and was invited by Florida's Governor Leroy Collins to work on issues affecting youth of Florida. The press was interested only in what I thought about integration of public schools. I could not imagine that there would be a credible argument against integration of public schools. I believed, even as a child, that we all come from the same Creator and we are equally human beings and spiritual beings. It was impossible for me to imagine segregation based on race, sex, or religion. I have not changed my beliefs. How will we ever learn about one another if we never face our differences without fear of reprisal? We must look at our differences in the glaring light of day, help people come out of bondage wherever it is and in whatever form it takes, and move on with our lives. As we show others the way, we come out of the bondages of our own lives. When I see Saudi women, I think of the old Chinese custom of binding women's feet in order to render them helpless. Surely, Saudi is one of the last countries set on stunting women's growth by keeping them under a stifling religious law that prevents them from being equals with men.

Every day I passed the same construction, saw the same wild traffic, and arrived at work to the same problems. One day I arrived at work and saw one of our drivers looking as if he was about to cry. His name was Mohammed Salah; he was a serious, kind, conscientious man. Like Leroy, he was Ethiopian, but unlike Leroy, he had a wife, a two year old, and a new baby. He had been up all night with his wife and their sick baby. I saw the hopelessness in his face. I prayed that the baby would recover from this illness, and I bought a gift for the other child. Often it was difficult to know how to help in terrible situations. One of the other drivers went to the hospital with a huge growth on his leg. A friend and I visited him in the hospital and brought him his favorite candy. In the hospital, he was wearing his same street clothes; I surmised that there were no hospital clothes, although hospital care, such as it is, is free in Saudi Arabia. Another day I came to work and heard shouting and screaming. Outside one of the gardeners was clubbing another gardener in the head with a hoe. Blood was streaming all over the place, as the victim laid on the walkway. His attacker ran away screaming and waving his arms in a frenzied fit.

Thanksgiving came and we went to the Desert Inn for Akmed's special Thanksgiving dinner which was delicious. We could see that we would be in Saudi until the following summer and that Allen would return to Saudi for Christmas vacation. I was happy that he would be coming home and was excited about decorating the house and getting Christmas gifts.

I did not care if I never organized another event! I was tired and wanted to spend more time at home with Preston and Chet and to prepare for Christmas when Allen would come for a three week visit. I could not imagine myself ever becoming a career person; my family meant too much to me. I agreed to work until the end of the year. My final work event was a Christmas party for the children. It was an all day long event with refreshments and special programs. Dr. Woodberry joined us and told the Christmas story, and we sang Christmas carols.

Afterwards, at work, I recommended a friend who was hired for my position. She died within a few months on Easter Sunday 1979 of a heart attack. Already, a dark cloud was forming across the Middle East. I would remember 1979 as the year of death and the dark cloud.

UNVEILINGS
A Desert Journey
by
Patricia Adora Clark Taylor

CHAPTER ELEVEN -- DARK CLOUDS GATHERING
Riyadh, Saudi Arabia -- 1979

1979 Riyadh – Desert Dust Storm Approaching Our Compound

In January, an order came down from the Saudi royal family declaring that we no longer could have Christian services, so we decided to meet in individual homes for worship. Dr. Woodberry sent the congregation a series of his printed sermons which he named "The Catacomb Letters." He visited in individual homes whenever possible to share in our worship.

In February, Chet flew home on the first available flight to Florida to attend the funeral of his stepfather who had been a blessing to Chet and to his mother. Chet flew out on the first available flight. I made arrangements for Preston and me to follow a day later on a military charter flight out of Dhahran. We flew from Riyadh to Dhahran for the connecting charter flight into Frankfurt, Germany where we would stay overnight before continuing on to the States. However, when we arrived at the airport in Dhahran our military charter flight was delayed in Dhahran. Islamic fundamentalism had raised its ugly head in Iran; the crisis in Iran meant that frantic Americans immediately were to be evacuated from Teheran. Therefore, our flight was put on stand-by in case it was needed to get Americans out of Teheran. We waited for several hours to see if the airplane would take off for Teheran or continue on to Frankfurt as planned. Preston and I sat in the airport in Dhahran on our way to a funeral in Florida wondering what would happen with our flight. Events were unfolding rapidly. During the hours we waited in the airport, the Middle East slipped away from a course towards westernization into the terror of Islamic fundamentalism.

During the hours in the Saudi airport, I remember hearing the news while people in the airport spoke excitedly. I was amazed that Iran was in crisis so quickly. A friend of ours recently had been on assignment in Iran and returned to Saudi exclaiming about Iran's successful efforts towards westernization. Suddenly new events unfolded as Iran's "progress" stopped dead in its tracks and did a total reversal, not because of military might, but because of religious ideas. Fanaticism, the dark side of any religion, was spreading its hand of death across Iran and into Saudi Arabia, as Khomeini, a fanatic religious leader, returned from exile in France. The Shaw of Iran was disposed and fled for his life. Khomeini immediately took iron fisted control and the country took giant steps backwards. Women, who were ordered to go under the obiya (long black body coverings), were the first to suffer. In Saudi, Khomeini's fanatic religious tape recordings were heard in the marketplace and throughout the country. Saudi was under a threat much greater than Iraq's military might. Insidious religious thought was taking an ugly hold on Saudi at the same time that thousands of people were rushing to escape Teheran's new leadership. At just that time, Preston and I were trying to get to Florida to attend a funeral!

After we sat for several hours at the Dhahran airport, our flight was released to fly on to Frankfurt where we witnessed people arriving from Teheran. It was such a frantic time in Frankfurt, and we did not know what would happen to our charter flight to the States. We waited at the airport military hotel for news of our charter flight. Finally, our plane left, but we were not told where the plane would land until we were in the air. During our flight, the pilot announced that we would land in South Carolina. There was one bright spot about that flight. One of the pilots was celebrating his birthday with a birthday cake. He invited Preston into the cockpit to have cake while getting a view from the cockpit. Preston decided then that he wanted to be a pilot! When we finally arrived in Jacksonville, we had been in route almost five days. The funeral was over and the guests had gone home, but Chet's mother was happy to see us! She was grateful that we made the effort to be with her and that we arrived safely. While we were in the States, I saw how tired Chet seemed; also, he was having chest pains. I accompanied him to the doctor for testing; all of his tests came back normal. However, my blood pressure was up, and I went to the hospital for a kidney test. Everything tested normal for me; I was glad I had no kidney problems!

Soon we were back in Saudi Arabia. This time I had no difficult projects facing me at work; I could relax and take life easier. During March and April, Chet was having chest pains accompanied by pain in his left arm. He had another EKG at the dispensary which showed everything to be normal. I was no longer working and was pleased that a woman who was enthusiastic about organizing events has replaced me. In April, on Easter Sunday at a planned desert event, the women who replaced me died suddenly of a heart attack! I could not believe she was dead; she had been so vibrant and full of life and excited about her new job. Shock waves went throughout the Corps community. Dark clouds of death seemed to hover all around me. The death of individuals close to me was intertwined in my thoughts about a dying middle east, strangling on a religious culture that refused to give way to modernity.

Chet and I continued to look forward to a departure date. Our plans were to leave Saudi in June; the furniture packing date was set for the first week in May. All was going as scheduled; our personal furniture items were packed and moved out of our house, temporary furnishings were moved in for our use. On May 15, Chet returned home from a morning tennis match in pain. His arm was hurting and the pain was getting worse. I called Linda, a friend of ours who had been a cardiac nurse in the States before coming to live in Saudi. She took one look at Chet and called her husband Henry who worked with Chet. Henry assisted Chet into a car and drove us to the dispensary where the male nurse assured Chet there was nothing wrong with him. The nurse did give Chet a shot for pain, but the pain got worse. Two hours later we drove Chet, who was in agony, to the newly constructed, modern Saudi Arabian Military Hospital and prayed that we would be able to get him into the hospital. The hospital was built for Saudi use; bed space generally was not available to Americans. We walked directly into the emergency room and said we needed help. Miraculously, the doctor on duty agreed to see us; he examined Chet and told us to come back in two days and see the head of the cardiology department. Against all odds, it appeared that we would get Chet into the hospital. We took Chet home and prayed for two days.

I called everyone I could think of and asked them to pray for Chet. I was remembering the woman who took my job, and how suddenly she died of a heart attack in April, only one month ago. Death seemed so close! I prayed that Chet would live and not die. After two days, we returned to the hospital with Chet and saw the head cardiologist who was British. He took one look at Chet and asked him how many cigarettes he smoked in a day. Chet admitted to three packs a day. The doctor told Chet to go outside and smoke his last cigarette ever. Then Chet was taken in a wheelchair up to the intensive care unit and put to bed. This section of the hospital was controlled by American and British medical heart teams working together. The cardiology section of this new hospital was important because King Khaled, who had heart disease, wanted to ensure that an outstanding staff always was available for any emergency. One medical team was the well known Seventh Day Adventist team from Loma Linda, California. This Christian medical team, consisting of several doctors and nurses, traveled around the world giving medical care to desperate people in remote places. At this time, the Loma Linda team was in Saudi Arabia especially for King Khaled, but the Saudis allowed the team to travel throughout Saudi Arabia and bring emergency cases to the hospital for treatment. I was told that heart disease is prevalent throughout Saudi Arabia, in part, because of marriage within families. Whatever their reasons for being here, I just was glad the team was in Saudi at this time. Here in the desert, Chet was getting excellent care; and the Loma Linda team, a likable, jovial group, was happy to have an English speaking patient! They enjoyed talking with Chet and reading his American newspapers and magazines.

In spite of the good care, Chet got worse and was having angina on a regular basis. The team did a heart catheterization and saw that Chet needed heart by-pass surgery immediately. They thought chances were good that Chet would not survive a trip back to the States for surgery. Dr. Rossi, the team's heart surgeon, spoke with Chet about this; and Chet agreed to have surgery. The night before surgery, the team prayed with Chet and me; also, Dr. Woodberry, who came often to visit Chet, had a private visit with him. The two of them prayed together and a peace came over Chet. Chet told me he was prepared to live or to die. At home, I tried to still Preston's fears and to let him know that everything would be all right. I decided to call Allen at school only when the surgery was over. That night I had my own private conversation with God and thanked Him for all the great blessings on our lives; I believed that Chet would live. I called Chet's mother; how much I dreaded that phone call! I told her that I would talk with her the next day about the surgery. I assured her that Chet had excellent care. I called my family and asked them and their friends to pray. I was exhausted, and I put a "Do Not Disturb" sign on the front door of our house. The next day, Dr. Woodberry and Roberta came to be with me during the surgery. I greatly appreciated their prayers and efforts on our behalf. I realized how much they meant to Chet and me and to so many others.

The triple by-pass surgery was successful. After surgery, the chief surgeon assured us that all went well, and that Chet had suffered no permanent damage from a heart attack. My friend Linda also stayed with me during the surgery; she was helpful with medical terminology, and it was good for me to have her by my side. The anesthesiologist spoke with me about the surgery which went well. He said, however, that no one could know how long Chet would live because his heart was in very poor condition. He said Chet could live for five years or twenty years; however, he thought Chet actually needed a heart transplant. Then the doctor turned his attention to me and spoke about my future. He encouraged me to begin building a life for myself, and we spoke about my returning to university classes when I returned to Maryland. Regarding Chet, he warned me that patients sometimes are different after going through this surgery and that Chet may be more agitated at times. He indicated that the road ahead would not be easy, then said to me, "You're the one I'm sorry for." I was surprised by his words, but I knew he meant what he told me. He was the oldest member of the team and was highly respected by all. He and his wife always traveled together; they were an intelligent, delightful pair. That day my life began to change as I considered what was ahead of me.

The next few weeks were painful times for Chet as he attempted to walk a few steps, then around his room, and finally down the hall and around the hospital floor. He made excellent progress which pleased everyone. By this time, Saudis patients on the floor (all men) had taken a real interest in Chet and me. Each time I left, they watched to see us kiss goodbye. Also, Chet and I held hands when we walked down the hallways. When we passed by Saudi men, they would stare at us. Holding hands with a woman was something strange to them!

Before Chet's surgery, Chet and I were introduced to Chet's new roommate. He was a Saudi boy about ten years of age with heart disease. The Loma Linda team had the boy flown from his village to the hospital where they planned to repair his heart with surgery. The boy was thrilled and told us in his broken English that, after his surgery, he would return to his village able to run and play like other boys. He was so excited! One day I came in to visit Chet, and I saw the boy sobbing with his head buried in his pillow. Chet told me the boy was unable to have his surgery because the hospital did not have his blood type. Chet wrote a note to the Corps of Engineers about the matter; soon there was more than enough blood for the child because Corps personnel lined up to give blood! The child's surgery and recovery was a bright spot during Chet's hospitalization! The young boy was with me during Chet's surgery and kept repeating, "How is Taylor?" Before Chet left the hospital, we watched as the boy ran down the hallway. Chet, too, made an astounding recovery while vowing to never smoke another cigarette. Finally, the day arrived when Chet returned to our home in the wadi compound after spending one month in the hospital; but, most of all, he wanted to return to America. He had been afraid of never seeing his homeland again.

At the end of June, we had a farewell party for the Bible Study Group, the hospital medical team, the Woodberry's, and other close friends. Everyone brought food for a buffet dinner. It was an evening of celebration as we brought to a close the events of our Saudi life including Chet's successful surgery. The party was our final event! We hugged everyone and said one last farewell prayer, thanking God for bringing us to this parting moment. The first week of July, Chet, Preston, and I boarded a Saudia Airlines flight out of Riyadh destined for New York. The doctors made a special request for first class travel for the three of us, so we were going home alive and in style! The plane lifted off the runway, and I gave a sigh of relief. For almost three years, we gave ourselves to Saudi Arabia; now we were going home with many memories of a bitter-sweet desert experience. Fourteen hours later, we arrived in New York; several hours later we were with family and friends in Jacksonville. Chet's mother met us at the airport and put her arms around Chet. It was a wonderful moment! After our Florida visit, we returned to our home on the Magothy River in Maryland. Chet eventually returned to work with the Corps of Engineers in Baltimore; Preston and Allen returned to school.

I remained interested in Middle East events and enrolled at the University of Maryland (UMBC) to complete a four year course in political science with emphasis on Middle East studies. As a result of Egyptian President Sadat's historic visit to Israel and the ensuing Camp David Peace Accords, the Sinai Desert was to be returned to Egypt by Israel. In the spring of 1981, Chet was recruited by the Corps to relocate with his family to Tel Aviv, Israel to build the peace keeping camps in the Sinai, part of the process to return land in the Sinai to Egypt. We were in agreement that going to Israel made sense for us and would be an education experience for Preston, now thirteen, and Allen, who soon would complete high school.

During our flight home from Saudi Arabia, I remembered Arabia and later wrote this poem:

A PICTURE OF ARABIA
by Patricia Adora Clark Taylor

Colors of amber, blue, and white
Houses of concrete or mud
Deserts of endlessly rolling sands
Sounds of laughter -- outrageous delight!
Women in gold, red dye on their hands
Regally dressed in black gauze-like robes
Some carrying babes and arms filled with goods
Men standing by in long flowing thobes.
A land that is blistered from rays of the sun
Parched, cracked, broken, and dry
Against a sun that is brilliant and blue
A contrast in texture, color, and hue.
A people resisting the change that they see
Who struggle and fight each day to exist
Arms lifted in prayer, strong hands exposed
For a future envisioned only through midst.
How will they be one hundred years hence
Caught up in a global race to survive
Their past gives a hint of a conquering race
Nomadic, intuitive, often alone -- but alive.
Some will follow the winds of the sea
Daughters who long to study afar
Their backs to the desert, their face to the sun
To Europe, to science -- the sky and the stars!
O daughters of sand and desert and dust
Come away and study and learn
Take of the best and grow to be wise
But sometimes for your past you will yearn.
Colors of amber, blue, and white
Houses of concrete or mud
Deserts of endlessly rolling sands
Sounds of laughter -- outrageous delight!

UNVEILINGS
A Desert Journey
by
Patricia Adora Clark Taylor

CHAPTER TWELVE -- ISRAEL AND BEYOND
Tel Aviv, Israel -- 1981

GALILEE

Chet, Preston, Allen, and I landed in Tel Aviv, Israel on October 4, 1981. When we arrived in the airport, Preston exclaimed, "This reminds me of Saudi Arabia," immediately noticing that Israel had a middle east flavor about it. Preston was not happy. We all thought Israel would be a more western nation. The truth is that Israel, modern in many ways, is centered in middle east history and culture and retains an eastern identity. Nevertheless, I was excited about being in Israel and tried to convey my excitement to Preston who was not excited about being taken out of a "normal" American school in Maryland, where he was making friends, and taken to another middle east country. Now he would attend the American School in Tel Aviv; Preston did not hide his disappointment!

Our trip over from the States was fairly uneventful even though our layover in Paris was extended from three hours to seven hours because of a labor strike in Italy and Yugoslavia. However, we finally arrived in Tel Aviv with our luggage about 8:30 p.m. Friday, October 2. We checked into our hotel on the Mediterranean Sea and finally got to sleep about midnight. The next morning we awoke to bright sunshine. I looked out from our hotel room window on the fourth floor to the beach and sparkling Mediterranean ocean just below us.

The day begins early in Tel Aviv with its sunny, warm climate. Bathers already were on the beach, and the city had come to life. We dressed and went down to buffet brunch which is served each Saturday in the hotel dining room. Saturday, rather than Sunday, is the holy day in Israel. The hotel dining room had an expansive ocean view. Allen and Preston immediately joined American friends from Riyadh who had been awaiting their arrival. Several Corps of Engineers families, formerly in Riyadh, were now in Tel Aviv. It was an exciting reunion!

The Tel Aviv hotel on the Mediterranean Sea, completely occupied by the Corps for offices and American employee residences, would be a kind of home for us even though Chet and I would have our own apartment in a nearby apartment building. The work that Chet would manage was the building of peace keeping camps in the Sinai for United Nations' Multi-National Forces who would occupy the Sinai and keep the peace during the land transition and afterwards. The camps would be like dots on the desert where young men from various nations would live and keep a watchful eye for problems. There was urgency about completing the project within the scheduled nine months, because the Egypt-Israel peace process was tied to a rigid time frame.

Israel, my first letter home, Wednesday, October 7, 1981
My first letter home, dated October 7, 1981, read, "Saturday afternoon, Chet and I walked several miles in our area of the city. The streets are tree-lined, and the block and stone construction is much like other parts of the Middle East. We looked in shop windows and stopped at a sidewalk cafe where we had a refreshing sparkling apple drink. Sitting outside the shop, we watched people strolling past us. Israelis remind me of Italians; Tel Aviv reminds me of Italy or of Alexandria in Egypt. Chet and I walked over to our new apartment; I was impressed with the location with trees all around and with adjacent shops. All in all, it is nice by American standards which makes it plush by Israeli standards.

Already I am making friends. Lilly Gerter is a neighbor in the apartment building. Her husband is head of the electrical program for the bases. They are a delightful Jewish couple from Boston. The next day, on Sunday, I went with Lilly and several other friends to see Tel Aviv University and walk around the campus. I located the Overseas Student Building, checked myself into the program, and learned that October 26 is when I receive my class schedule. I am excited to get started with classes! The campus is modern looking and lush and green with many palm trees. Everyone was in tee shirts, shorts, and sandals. It is my kind of place!

Chet was gone on Sunday and Monday to Sharm-el-Shiek by the Red Sea at the tip of the Sinai to meet with Israeli and Egyptian military personnel about preparations for construction of the peace keeping bases. Chet was pleased to see that everyone was friendly and prepared to get on with the process. At one point the Israeli officer asked the Egyptian officer if Israelis would still be allowed to come into the seaside tourist area of Sharm-el-Sheik after return of the land to Egypt. The Egyptian officer laughed and answered, "Of course, but we will run the businesses and make the money!" At this time, the Israelis own the tourist facilities and have built a lucrative tourist area for vacationing locals and Europeans. However, I read in yesterday's newspaper that, because Israelis can no longer operate businesses on land after the land return in April, they are considering investment in ships that will cruise in the sea for deep sea fishing. I believe good business people will find opportunity in every event!

On Monday, a friend took Preston and me to the American International School to enroll Preston and get him started in his classes. The school is British run but has an American academic format. Most of the school's instructors seem to be Jewish American. The person who organized Preston's schedule is a young Jewish woman from Chevy Chase, Maryland who went to University of Maryland. She, like all the instructors we met, was very friendly. The school's atmosphere is casual with small classrooms. The relaxed but orderly atmosphere reminded me of Allen's private school in Florida, the Vanguard School. Several of the teachers were in shorts and sandals; the relaxed atmosphere helped put Preston at ease. As it turns out, Preston likes the school. It is good he knows students who helped him feel at home and fit into the swing of things.

Yesterday was Tuesday, and I spent the day in Jerusalem with Lilly and several friends. Father Philip, a Franciscan priest, was our tour guide and gave an outstanding tour. Lilly, who is Jewish, enjoyed the tour very much because Father Philip spoke a great deal about the Jewish faith and referred often to the fact that Jesus was a young Jewish man. Lilly and I sat with Father Philip at lunch and had a lively discussion about Judaism, Christianity, and Saudi Arabia. It was educational and fun! We arrived back at the hotel at 6 p.m.; that's when Chet and I heard the news that President Sadat had been killed. I felt terrible about it. I thought immediately of our Egyptian friends and their strong support for Sadat. I honestly felt crushed! You know the strong feeling I have for the Egyptians; I will never forget my visit with them in April of 1978 when there was so much excitement in the air about Sadat and his peace initiatives. All the talk here among our friends is simply speculation about Begin's reaction and the consequences for the base programs. The American attitude is "business as usual" and "full steam ahead" unless otherwise notified. Even if the contracts should suddenly terminate, we would be here several more months in order to close them out. However, I imagine that Began will want the bases completed regardless of the outcome of the peace treaty. If nothing else, Israel will end up with additional bases.

Allen is enjoying our stay at the hotel. He has met everyone from the young Israeli guards to the cooks in the kitchen. He has job applications in several places and should soon have a job. He met two young Canadians who work at Ramon Air Base; Allen hopes to go there. In the meanwhile, he is enjoying himself. Every time I see him, he is with a group of young people. I am reading up on Palestine history in the twentieth century. I am glad I studied Middle East History at University of Maryland; it helps set the stage for all this information. Also, I am glad for my Middle East study in Saudi and in Italy.

P.S. Thursday, October 8 -- Last night was Yom Kippur Eve and no cars were allowed on the streets. Chet and I walked for a long time through the streets where children were biking and playing. Many families and couples were out walking; it was delightful. There was a festive feeling in the air in spite of the shock of Sadat's death. Earlier I had walked along the beach and noticed that the soldiers were wearing steel helmets instead of their berets. A friend with me asked the soldiers if they were expecting any trouble; they replied that they hoped not.

Today is Yom Kippur. Chet and I will walk among the crowds and take in as much of the city as possible.

Israel, my second letter home, October 18, 1981
We all are well and very much into Israeli life. Chet, Allen, Preston, and I went with another family to Jerusalem and Jericho for a full and interesting day. Freddie, our driver and guide, was a survivor of the Polish holocaust. He came to Israel in the early 1950s at the age of fifteen. Freddie drove us along a route to Jerusalem that, in certain places along the way, is dotted with old armored vehicles from Israeli convoys burned up during the Six Day War when Israel recaptured Jerusalem and entered it as victors for the first time in two thousand years. All during the day, Freddie's explanations of surrounding landscapes went like this, "Here is where King David did (so and so); here is where Israel did (such and such) during the Six Day War." In Jerusalem, we heard more about the Six Day War and at Jericho we heard still more. It is a war that still lives in the minds of Israelis. The 1973 War is spoken of from time to time, but mostly we heard about the glory of the Six Day War.

Chet is busy at meetings with Israeli military personnel, embassy officials, etc. He is surrounded with millions of details involved in laying the foundation for this program. Secretly, he is calling it "Mission Impossible." Our household goods are tied up in customs; the Israeli general in charge of the program told Chet the release of the household goods will have to be approved by the Knesset, which is the Israeli parliament. How amazing!

I am happy to be here. Preston enjoys school; his only problem is a long bus trip because it makes so many stops to get children at different Tel Aviv locations. Preston will do just fine; he has a history of school bus experiences! He looks forward to a two day school trip with his classmates on November 1 to the Sea of Galilee. Yesterday he and Chet visited the Sea of Galilee with other friends. I rested up from a full week of touring and getting ready for classes. Chet and Preston learned much about Capernaum, Megiddo, and the valley of Megiddo also known as the valley of Armageddon. On

Monday, October 12th, I went with friends to tour the Dead Sea area, Jericho, and Masada. It was a long day's tour. We took a cable car to the top of Masada which is 1300 feet above the Dead Sea. We were told Masada is just about sea level. It was hot and dry at the top, but the excavations were interesting. Israeli soldiers with machine guns had a bunker there. Once more it was the story of the historic past and the uncertain present and future. Later we stopped for an hour at the Dead Sea for a swim, actually for a float among huge clumps of salt that can be held in both hands. Everyone floats in the Dead Sea because of the buoyancy. The water in the Dead Sea is perfectly still and is a deep blue-green color. Swimmers floating in the sea stay in one spot because of the water's stillness. The sea is brilliant against gold-brown mountains and bright blue sky. I was told that one of the European governments sponsors some people with skin diseases to come here for treatment.

On Thursday I went to Jerusalem. By coincidence it was a Jewish pilgrim day; there was bumper to bumper traffic. At Mt. Moriah, which is the location of Islam's Dome of the Rock, orthodox Jews were trying to keep people out, even throwing stones, because they believe the glory of God was manifested at the holy spot. In Biblical times, the Jewish temple with its Holy of Holies was located on the mount. Orthodox Jews only travel as far as the wailing wall. They will go no further for fear of being struck dead by God. Earlier, when Chet and I went to Jerusalem, we could not go on Mt. Moriah because it was a Moslem holy day. Some holy days are designated for Moslems; other holy days are designated for Jews. I suppose it is just as well that the ultra Orthodox Jews and the Moslems do not come face to face on top of Mt. Moriah. What an encounter that might be! Anyway, between the religious "holy day" restrictions of Arabs and Jews, I have not been to the Dome of the Rock since we came to live in Israel.

On Friday, I went with Father Philip, the Franciscan priest, and with friends in a private car tour of Jerusalem. Father Philip is a kind of personal guardian for Americans in the Multi-National Forces program. He is skilled in working with Catholics, Protestants, and Jews. He drove us to Bethlehem, Mount of Olives, Gethsemane, and the old city of Jerusalem. He had keys to private entrances so we avoided the crowds of bus tourists. He took us through back alleyways and opened doors that were closed to the public. From 1975 to 1978, Father Philip studied as a priest in the inner city; he knew many unusual facts. While living in Jerusalem, he also was a charismatic Bible study instructor for a non-denominational study group. Father Philip believes that Israel must not be blinded by past victories but must be vigilant in order to perceive the entire Middle East picture correctly and to adjust accordingly. He believes that Israel needs modern day prophets.

Today is October 20th, Tuesday, and a Succoth (feast of tabernacles) holiday. It is a Jewish celebration of the ingathering or harvesting. Tonight Preston and I are going to a Succoth celebration where Orthodox Jews kick up their heels and celebrate with song and dance. It should be quite festive! I hear it is the one day of the year when everyone really gets lively!

Last night Chet came in from work shaking his head in dismay and exclaiming, half kidding, that he did not know that he was going to renegotiate the Camp David agreement. He was in talks again yesterday with Israeli General Sion about fundamental philosophy regarding the peace camps. Chet now is studying the peace accord from some of my text books from middle east college courses. Also, as I read the newspapers, I make a mental note of any articles that I think he should read. We are a good team.

Today is Wednesday, the 21st. Yesterday I was reading about Moshe Dayan's life. Since his death on Friday and his burial on Sunday, much has been written about him. I would like to read some of the books he wrote about his life. One of his daughters is married to General Sion who works with Chet. Her name is Yael, and she is a well known poet.

Yesterday over lunch, Chet asked me how I would like to do a semester at Tel Aviv University followed by a semester at Cairo University. He was serious, and I answered that I would like it just fine. It seems that in April, when the peace camps become operational, the Israelis suggested that the Corps of Engineers finish their business in Cairo. The finishing up work will consist of closing out contracts and tying up any loose ends; sometimes it can be a drawn out procedure. I am glad I am keeping notes. This could prove to be interesting. During lunch, we were with other Corps of Engineer officials who were joking about meetings with Israelis. Apparently at the first meeting, they entered a room with an American flag on one side of a long table and an Israeli flag on the other side. The Americans lined up on one side of the table and their Israeli counterparts lined up on the other side. Then they sat down and spent a moment of silence staring at one another. As engineers who will build the camps, they all have been left with the job of clarifying exactly how the camps are to be used and for what purposes. There was a US State Department official present, but he did not say a word; later he offered Chet advice about what should have been said by the engineers.

Chet is frustrated today. He says he can't seem to get a handle on this program, and he cannot see where it is going. I hope that better days are ahead. However, Chet is doing a good job. He is admired and respected. Someone said to me today, "You are married to "the" Chet Taylor?!"

Today is Saturday, 24th of October. Colonel Lee, whom Chet works for in this program, just returned from a couple of weeks in the States. Last night, at the hotel, he came to the table where we were eating dinner and told Chet he had word that the Egyptians were going to provide the electrical part of the program by purchasing it from the Israelis. The peace camps will be at Sharm-el-Sheik and Etom Air Base where there are facilities now used by Israelis.

We are in the process of moving into our apartment which we enjoy very much. We have a view of the city and can see the Mediterranean Sea. We are stretched out and relaxed in the living room. Preston and Allen went to the Palace Hotel for brunch. Chet and I are about to go to Joppa to walk through the old city area.

End of Letters Home; Beginning of Tel Aviv University Study

I continued to be shocked by the death of Egyptian President Anwar el-Sadat who was assassinated by Muslim extremists during a military parade commemorating the 1973 Yom Kippur War against Israel. The assassins, posing as soldiers in the military procession, attacked Sadat's reviewing stand with machine guns and grenades. And my heart went out to Chet who was here to manage a project which may not come to pass. I knew Chet, who made a remarkable recovery from heart surgery, wanted to complete this project and wanted it to be successful. No one knew what would happen. The Israeli people put their great hope for peace in Egypt's President Sadat and trusted him to keep his word about the peace process. Now Egypt's President Sadat was dead, and Israel and Egypt mourned his death. Once again, death clouds hovered around us! Shortly afterwards, on October 16, one of Israel's hero's, General Moshe Dayan, died in Tel Aviv of cancer. Again, Israel was stunned and saddened. General Dayan was an Israeli military warrior who became a crusader for peace. He was skilled in both battle and diplomacy. His death was viewed as huge loss for Israel and for peace.

The month of October continued to be riddled with emergencies. Suddenly, I was struck down with a painful bleeding cyst on one of my ovaries; and I was hospitalized for surgery. The problem was corrected; I quickly recovered and began classes at Tel Aviv University. Meanwhile, newspaper headlines around the world announced middle east events daily; and rumors spread throughout Israel hourly. In the midst of blaring news, Chet received word to continue on as planned with construction of the peace keeping camps in the Sinai.

We moved into a high-rise Tel Aviv apartment building near Chet's office, not far from Tel Aviv University or from Preston's school, the International American School. During any spare time we had as a family, we hired a private guide and visited sites holy to Christians, Jews, and Moslems. Within a short time, Allen secured a job working for the Corps of Engineers at Ramon Air Base as a GS 1. Allen, the low man on the totem pole, had an interesting job running errands for the Colonel in charge. He had a chance to interact with Ramon's personnel, and he became friends with a number of the young Israeli pilots. In the morning he would see A-4s and F-16s lined up on the runway and watch as his friends flew out of sight on practice missions. Preston, in spite of earlier protests, enjoyed meeting students from different parts of the world and studying international events.

At Tel Aviv University, I joined classes taught in English with a number of other students from the States; most of them were Jewish. A few, like me, were not Jewish but were interested in middle east studies and were gaining college credits while attending a foreign university. To complete my University of Maryland junior year requirements, I took five courses in the fall semester and five courses in the spring semester. My course work involved Israel's political, economic, and social history together with a broad spectrum of contemporary middle east classes, including petroleum politics and petroleum economics. I worked diligently to study the materials, to complete my research at Tel Aviv University's library, and to write essays that reflected my study and my ideas. I made friends with other American students.

At the time, about five hundred Palestinian students attended Tel Aviv University. They heard that I lived in Saudi Arabia, and some were curious to know about my life in Saudi. We spent long hours discussing the middle east and the conflict that affected their entire lives. In spite of wars and rumors of wars, they were an optimistic group. One of the Palestinian students was in love with a student from New York. She was young, but serious and mature. I found him to be intelligent and polite with a sense of humor. He grew up on a nearby farm with his parents and a dozen brothers and sisters. An English Literature major, his dream was to write poetry about love and life and war and peace. The young New Yorker and the young Palestinian had no one to talk with about their love affair, and so they spoke with me; I listened with interest.

Later, when General Sharon invaded Lebanon, the young Palestinian and his brothers wanted to be part of the Israeli forces; but they were forbidden by the Israelis. The Israeli rejection was a crushing blow for them. The 1982 invasion of Lebanon changed young Palestinian Israelis' attitudes and deepened cultural and political differences. It seemed to me that the Lebanese Invasion was a war which strongly divided the Israeli public and worsened the overall conflict.

TEL AVIV UNIVERSITY STUDENTS

The Palestinian group wanted me to join them for an afternoon at one of their universities, recently closed by the Israeli government. I agreed to go, in part, because my advisor, Dr. Louis Cantori, at the University of Maryland had encouraged me to get out among the people to learn different views of political issues and, if possible, to visit the Arab university. The now closed university looked old and dusty and was dotted with bullet holes which the group eagerly pointed out to me. We walked to a nearby cafe for tea and talked about politics.

The topics could have been discussed on any Stateside college campus; but here it meant more because these were the people enveloped by the conflict. They walked, talked, lived, and breathed the Arab-Israeli conflict and the idea of a Palestinian homeland. I tried to get outside my Caucasian American self, but there was no way I could enter their world and understand the depth of their desire for a restored homeland. All I could do was listen to their opinions, their hopes, and their dreams.

I did know that it was important for me to understand all I could about the Palestinians who were a key to the Arab-Israeli conflict. My Tel Aviv learning experience had to spill out of the classroom, away from textbooks, and into the life of the people. One of my courses, Arab-Israeli Conflict, was taught by Professor Itamar Rabinovich who later became Israel's ambassador to the United States. His intellectual work was respected and his course covered all aspects of Arab-Israeli Conflict. At the end of the two semester coursework, during an exam, I would be required to write a peace plan for the region solid in its strategy and reasoning. I wanted to write a well-researched, creative, and rational paper.

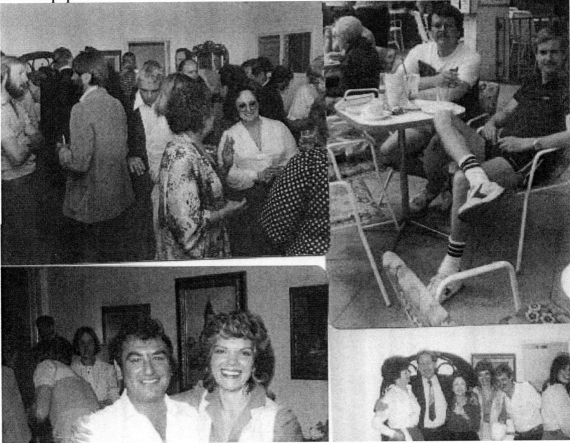

HOLIDAY PARTY AT OUR TEL AVIV APARTMENT

UPPER RIGHT, CHET WITH ENGINEER JOHN BAUMAN

Israel was such a huge learning experience. Back in my apartment, I would study in the afternoon, or evenings, or on weekends. Actually, I studied whenever I could find quiet time; but there were plenty of reasons not to study quietly all the time. Israel, itself, was the classroom. Chet, Allen, Preston, and I were learning history and politics from visiting historical sites, from the people we met, and from one another. Chet's classroom was his work; he and I had long discussions about Israel and the UN peacekeeping mission. One day Chet would meet with Israeli generals, another day he would meet with Egyptians. Preston, too, had his work cut out for him; he had papers to write and subjects to learn. Allen, now working at Ramon Air Base, was meeting modern-day Israeli warriors who were young, intelligent, and in top physical condition. Towards the end of our stay in Israel, Allen was offered a job working in Tel Aviv to transport mail to Multi-National Forces in the Sinai. He quickly accepted and soon was flying by the seat of his pants in a jeep through the desert. He interacted with Israeli guards, Egyptian guards, and the youthful Multi-National Forces stationed in the Sinai as he drove back and forth across militarized borders delivering the mail. Young, big, strong, tenacious, and gregarious, Allen was the perfect mail person! The Sinai was the classroom in which Allen excelled!

I had a number of Israeli friends including the doctor who saved my bleeding ovary early in my Israel stay. His name was Dr. Ron Rozen, and in a taxi on the way to his office, while in excruciating pain, I heard from the Corps nurse accompanying me that Dr. Rozen was one of the best doctors and surgeons in Israel. I first met the doctor when I walked into his office in pain, forced a smile, and introduced myself while extending my hand for a handshake. Dr. Rozen, about fifty, was tall and broad shouldered with a great tan and the clearest blue eyes I have ever seen. His great smile reassured me and he listened intently as I described my pain. While contacting Chet, he arranged for me to be taken to a nearby private hospital and put into the loveliest wing of the hospital -- the maternity wing. My private room even had a private outside patio. By the time I got to the hospital, I almost was screaming in pain. I was examined and taken into surgery. Finally, I was out of pain! When I awoke, Chet and Preston were in the room with me and were happy to know that I would be just fine. Within a day or so, I was asking when I could begin my classes and was told to rest before starting classes.

Dr. Rozen stopped by often, and we enjoyed talking about my interest in middle east studies and my life in Saudi Arabia. After my hospital stay, we remained friends; he became an important person for helping me see war through the eyes of someone who has been there. In December he joined our family and friends for a Christmas "tree decorating" party where we all were on a first name basis. Our apartment was filled with Americans and Israelis. Everyone helped decorate our artificial tree from the States. One of my professors who taught petroleum history and economics stopped by with his wife. Everyone had a great time!

Dr. Rozen, now Ron to us, was kind enough to show me Israel through his eyes. I saw where he grew up near Jerusalem, and the places he loved to visit. His father's family came to Israel from Russia; his father became a doctor in Israel. Ron said he could remember, while as a child, trying to sleep at night in his upstairs bedroom as his father cared for patients downstairs who came to their door. Israelis or Arabs, they were cared for as individuals. I was intrigued by this man, and hoped that one day we all would meet under different circumstances.

One of the last times I saw him, he was caring for the wounded at a hospital in the hills between Jerusalem and the Lebanese border. It was just days after the Lebanese invasion began, and I had driven to where my dear friend was caring for others. In June, General Sharon had invaded Lebanon; this was Ron's fifth war, and he had two sons who went in this war. Each time a helicopter landed at the hospital with wounded, he and the other doctors and staff looked to see if there were any familiar faces. They dreaded to see the wounded who were flown in from the war. The hilltop hospital's parking lot was filled with people, many looked as if they were Palestinian mothers and fathers. I asked Ron about the danger of their being right there in the parking lot; he answered that the Palestinians came to get news of the war, especially about anyone wounded.

It was early afternoon, and Ron was able to leave the hospital for an hour. There was a place he wanted me to see. He gave me directions, and I drove us to a compound surrounded by a wire fence. He told me not to speak; he did not want anyone to know that I was an American. He would introduce me as a Canadian writer. Inside the compound, we entered a long, narrow one story structure with hospital beds lined along one wall. In each bed was a Syrian pilot, blindfolded. Ron brought me here to show me that Israelis do not harm prisoners of war. He explained that they are cared for until they can be exchanged for Israeli prisoners of war. He further explained that none of the Syrian pilots had been shot down. The pilots, flying Soviet aircraft which was not as modern as the Israeli aircraft, ejected immediately when they saw an Israeli fighter plane. The ejection device did not work properly; each of the bed ridden pilots had broken shoulders. I looked down at beautiful young men, all in a row in hospital beds, alone and away from home. I could only think of how worried their families must be!

There was no pride in Ron's voice about captured prisoners; there was only fatigue. I knew what was unspoken; Ron wanted to show me this place because it was his hope that one day, I might make a difference. Afterwards, we drove to a mountain village, the home of artists, and looked out at a panoramic view of the Sea of Galilee. He said to me, "When I die, do you think I will go to heaven?" I told him I knew he would surely be in heaven one day with me and with all our loved ones. Then I said, "Promise me that one day, when there is peace, we will return to this place." He promised me that one day we would return. I drove him back to the hospital and watched him walk away. I drove back to Tel Aviv.

Beyond Israel
Days afterwards, our Israel stay was completed; Chet's job was a great success! I completed all my exams and essays and was pleased with my grades. Preston completed his school work and said goodbye to his many friends. We returned to the States; and Chet, Preston, Allen, and I began to walk different roads. Allen stayed on in Israel, lived on a kibbutz for a year, and worked with Israelis. Preston entered public school and

continued with an interest in world events, aviation, and sports. I graduated with honors from University of Maryland and went to work on Capitol Hill for a Member of Congress. Later I completed graduate work at Duke University.

Ron and I corresponded as friends; he died of lung cancer several years after I left Israel. Chet died of heart disease in Dallas, Texas while working for the Corps of Engineers in 1997. Looking back, I realize that God has given me an extraordinary life! One day I hope I will come together with friends and loved ones on a mountaintop near the Sea of Galilee and we will live forever in peace.

PEACEKEEPERS IN THE SINAI -- SOLDIERS, PEACEKEEPER LEADERS, AND THE DESERT SOLDIERS WHO MAKE IT WORK -- THIS SUCCESSFUL PEACE INITIATIVE REMAINS TODAY!

**TOP LEFT AND RIGHT -- CHILDREN OF THE SINAI IN
A DESERT PLACE WHERE MOSES ONCE TRAVELED
AND RECEIVED THE TEN COMMANDMENTS**

**BOTTOM LEFT -- COLONEL LEE, AN OUTSTANDING LEADER, HEADING
UP THE CORPS OF ENGINEERS' WORK IN THE SINAI**

**BOTTOM RIGHT -- ROADWAYS THROUGH THE SINAI -- IF ONLY THE
ROCKS COULD SPEAK!**

ME AND CHET -- COMPLETING THE END OF THE JOURNEY

EACH OF US RECEIVED A LETTER OF RECOGNITION AND THANKS FROM COLONEL LEE FOR CONTRIBUTING TO "PEACE IN THE MIDDLE EAST"

BEGINNING THE JOURNEY IN ITALY IN 1973 WHERE PRESTON ROAD HIS BIKE DAILY, AL LOOKED FORWARD TO VISITS, CHET'S MOTHER TOOK SUMMER TRIPS WITH US --

NONE OF US KNEW WHAT WOULD BE REQUIRED OF US ON THE JOURNEY, BUT IT WAS WORTH IT ALL!
MY CHILDREN GREW UP FACING INTERNATIONAL CHALLENGES.
THEY BRAVELY DID ALL THAT WE REQUIRED OF THEM.
THEY, ALSO, CONTRIBUTED TO PEACE IN THE MIDDLE EAST!

**PRESTON'S HIGH SCHOOL GRADUATION IN 1986 --
ME, PRESTON, AL, AND CHET**

UNVEILINGS
A Desert Journey
by
Patricia Adora Clark Taylor

CHAPTER 13 – TRANSITIONS

1976 Riyadh – Camels in the Desert

My Middle East journey taught me about the agony of war, about the resiliency of the human spirit to journey onward, about the commonalties of the human race, about the loneliness, the quietness, and the beauty of the desert, and about the continuity of time. Yesterday is today and today is yesterday. In the Middle East there is a kind of fading in and out of centuries and even thousands of years – all within a few seconds. Love, war, jealousy, greed, and power provide the underlying theme. From the time Cain killed Able, we just keep on doing it to one another. Walls go up, walls are trodden down. Soldiers kill and establish their rule only to have other soldiers from another army come in and kill them and take their place. Nations rise and nations fall. War, death, misery, honor, and valor all ride the same horse. Each warring side has their cheering section and their detractors. Everyone is a pawn in the game of life being lived out on a stage. Shakespeare has it right! Even the "greats" like Alexander the Great, who conquered much of the known world a few hundred years before the time of Jesus, faded from the scene of life – no one is spared!

I am back to the historic Jesus. In all of history, he is the one who has the most extraordinary story. Even in the historic company of Alexander the Great, all the "greats" of the Roman Empire, the mighty Egyptian rulers, and the historic figures of Babylon, Jesus is the one who wins; he is not conquered by politicians or by soldiers or by the religious elite. He is not conquered by death and never fades from the scene. His life and his spirit of love permeates the human race and continues to find a home in the hearts of individuals. I am comforted by the fact that Jesus was not a warrior and that he did not die in a blaze of glory defending some group of people within some real or imaginary wall or boundary. Jesus was much too real for war. He was a man of peace who loved people and despised only self-righteous religion with all its propaganda, its twisted rhetoric, its politics, its wars, and its desire for profit at the expense of individuals. Jesus, who walked among men, women, and children, was nonchalant about Roman politics, but he was passionate about the evil of religious politics. He referred to his religious critics as vipers.

Jesus understood that religion could be the most dangerous part of human life. Jesus was accused of blasphemy because his own Jewish background and brilliant understanding of the Jewish scriptures threatened the religious teaching of others in high positions of leadership. Some of the religious leaders, fearing his popularity with the people and his teachings about loving God and neighbors and about being one with God, were horrified by this man who spoke such things. The Roman government found no fault in Jesus. No government ever killed Jesus; only fervent religious leaders were up to the task. Of course, there is another story surrounding his death. Simply stated, the story as told in the New Testament of the Bible, says that the goodness and the sanctity of Jesus neutralized and overcame the evil in each of us as his own blood was poured out in sacrifice. In spite of it all, Jesus lives! If we reach for him and for the goodness of his life, we will find that he already has prepared a way for us to come to him.

It was no accident that Jesus was a Jew. During his life, his followers were Jews. The scriptures were written by Jews. The early church was established by Jews. Jesus was born into an intelligent, ancient race of people who were brilliant writers, diligent in their work, and who kept meticulous ancient records. Throughout thousands of years the Jewish people have given so much to science, literature, medicine, the arts; and Jesus was their great gift to the world. I have a real love for Israel and the Jewish people. As I see it, the problem for Israel was that Jesus was not a warrior who would conquer their oppressors and lead them to the pinnacle of earthly power. Jesus was born into a world ruled by greed and in love with war and great warriors. Jesus was, himself, under a veil. The fact that Jesus emerged as a man of peace was an insult to many. How could this be? Surely it was true that, at his birth, kings of the world bowed before him and brought him priceless gifts of gold and silver and fragrances and spices. All the signs were right for Israel's great leader to appear. As the story continues, Satan offered Jesus the kingdoms of the world. The dark force of humanity wanted a new conquering warrior and ruler to worship him and to fly with him upon the winds of war. Jesus turned it down. He wanted no part of a physical earthly kingdom.

It is possible that Jesus was the greatest surprise of all time – and the greatest disappointment to some. He refused an earthly kingdom while prophesying destruction for Jerusalem. At the same time, during the Sermon on the Mount, as written in the sixth chapter of Matthew, Jesus identified the winners in his spiritual kingdom. Basically, they were the kind and good people; they were the people of peace. Later he died on a cross, high and lifted, perhaps upon the threshing rock overlooking Jerusalem. Then surprise of surprises, Jesus reappeared and walked among the people. He overcame death and opened the gates of heaven to every one of us, regardless of race or gender. Today Jesus speaks to each of us, "Come and follow me."

When I arrived back in the United States in the summer of 1982, I was like a fish out of water. I didn't feel that I belonged anywhere anymore; maybe I did not belong on planet Earth. I especially despised the racial divide and race politics. I found myself completing my university studies, including a study of Arabic language at Morgan State University in Baltimore and at the Middle East Institute in Washington, D.C. Later, I worked on Capitol Hill with Members of Congress and the outstanding staff associated with the Congressional Black Caucus. My actions were not born from a rebellious attitude; rather, they were born out of a genuine desire to tear down barriers that kept me from the reality of what the human race is and what it can accomplish as we work together.

I was forever branded by this Jesus; I went looking for him, and he found me. I related to the song of Mary (Luke 1: 46-55) when she was told she would have a child, *"My soul doth magnify the Lord, and my spirit hath rejoiced in God my savior. For he hath regarded the low estate of his handmaiden: for, behold, from henceforth all generations shall call me blessed. For he that is mighty hath done great things; and holy is his name. And his mercy is on them that fear him from generation to generation. He hath showed strength with his arm; he hath scattered the proud in the imagination of their hearts. He hath put down the mighty from their seats, and exalted them of low degree. He hath filled the hungry with good things; and the rich he hath sent empty away. He hath helped his servant Israel in remembrance of his mercy; as he spoke to our fathers, to Abraham, and to his seed forever..."* Undoubtedly, Mary's song was for all, but it has a special meaning for all the seed of Abraham and for women everywhere. The song has a rhythm, a motion that rises and falls and rises and falls. It is felt in the heart and deep in the belly. It has a continuity that extends from one generation to another. It's all about falling and being lifted up; falling and being lifted up.

My Middle East journey changed me for all time; it ended with the beginning of my stateside journey which would continue into the 1990s and into a new millennium. Bit by bit, the shroud was discarded; I walked into a new destiny. Much like two continents colliding in the long ago past; I set my feet upon new ground. Then, for a long time, I thought I lost my way. Actually, I was adjusting to new territory as I stepped upright into a new painting.

Once more, like Alice in Wonderland, I was seeing through a glass darkly…But, over time, because of my Middle East experience, I would begin to see with clarity.

USA
Capitol Hill Interns
Calling Family and Friends
September 11, 2001

SECTION THREE
Unveiled

And now abides faith, hope, love,
These three; But the greatest of these is love.
1 Corinthians 13: 13

<u>**UNVEILINGS**</u>
<u>*A Desert Journey*</u>
by
Patricia Adora Clark Taylor

THE OTHER SIDE OF THE DESERT
Pasadena, Maryland, 2003

MY GRANDSON STARNES AND ME, CHRISTMAS 2003

In the photo above, I am standing with my grandson who will be thirteen years of age in 2004. It is wonderful to see Starnes growing up and to talk with him about his life and the things that interest him. Suddenly it seems, I find myself in a day of computers and electronic games. How can this be? It was only yesterday that I was watching Preston ride his bike in Italy. It was only yesterday that I was writing stories on a manual typewriter in the desert. Where did the years go; how did I get to this place in my life?

After Israel, my life continued on without the many friends that I clung to in times past. I was out of touch with Patti Arcari and my other desert friends for years. My closest friend had been my husband Chet, but several years after returning to the States our lives began to separate. More and more, my life centered around my studies and my work on Capitol Hill where I worked with the well known (and recently deceased) Member of Congress Charles Bennett from Jacksonville, Florida. Mr. Bennett knew me when I was sixteen years old and was "Florida Governor of Girls State" in 1958. In 1984, he decided to hire me as his legislative assistant. I remember his words well, "I have never worked with a women legislative assistant, but I believe I can work with you."

Determined to do a good job, I assisted Mr. Bennett in writing effective legislation to create Jacksonville's now famous Timucuan Preserve within the National Park Service. It was initiated at a time when the Reagan administration wanted to get rid of some park lands; but, in the end, our legislation was so well written and our research was so thorough, that the legislation passed as a stand alone bill!

It was a unique legislative effort because of the many books which Congressman Bennett had written on north Florida history. At our first Congressional Hearing in 1984 before the House Subcommittee on Parks and Recreation, chaired by Congressman Bruce Vento, Mr. Bennett had me place seven books (which he authored on north Florida history) on the podium in front of Mr. Vento. It was an unforgettable beginning to extensive testimonies from expert witnesses about the great need to preserve some of north Florida's pristine wetlands and fascinating early Timucuan Indian and French history. Mr. Bennett had high regard for the Timucuan Indian nation and wanted the Indian name attached to the preserve. Mr. Bennett was a most remarkable person; he survived for forty-four years in the US House of Representatives. He walked with two canes and with braces on both legs. He never complained, and he attended every necessary hearing and listened to each word of testimony. He was the ranking member of the powerful House Armed Services Committee, but never chaired the Committee because (in my judgment) other Members, fearing his strict moral ethics and his rigorous dedication to duty, refused to elect him as their Chairman .

While I was working on Capitol Hill, Chet wanted to move away; he decided to take a job in Dallas. I tried to cling to life as it had been and followed Chet to Texas. Within a couple of days of arriving in Texas, I met Ross Perot and began working for Electronic Data Systems' (EDS) banking industry group located in Plano, Texas. I traveled from one end of the US to the other calling on (the then) "big eight" accounting firms. EDS was considering partnering with such a firm for large systems integration projects. The idea was that EDS would integrate large, complex systems while the partner firm handled any problems associated with human relations, employee education, and employee restructuring. In the end, EDS decided to create its own "partner firm" as an in-house department. Additionally, I introduced Federal Reserve Banks across the nation to EDS accomplishments in system integration, hosted an EDS seminar for Federal Reserve Bank officials, and assisted EDS in responding to a proposal request from the Federal Reserve Bank of Philadelphia.

By 1988, Chet and I had come to an impasse in our marriage. We divorced in the summer of 1988 while declaring our "forever friendship." I eventually moved back to Capitol Hill, but not before living in North Carolina and completing graduate work at Duke University. I was curious about the effect of science and religion on culture. My final paper was written about Professor Mohammed Abdus Salam who won the Nobel Prize for Theoretical Physics in the 1970s. He was a Pakistani physicist who kept a photo of Einstein on his desk and followed in Einstein's professional footsteps. In the paper, I followed the life of Abdus Salam through the partition of India, the creation of Pakistan, through his life in British schools and Moslem madrassas (schools) and his brilliant work at Cambridge University. He also won an Atoms for Peace award and is, perhaps, still alive today and working in Italy.

Regarding my paper, the question which interested me: "Was Abdus Salam more eastern or more western in his thought?" I found the answer in one of his books in which he mentioned that his Islam was large enough to encompass all that he could possibly learn and all that was encompassed by the universe. Islam, together with his eastern thought, was the core of who he was and the wellspring for his immense knowledge. Abdus Salam's western teachings only enlarged his eastern beliefs. He was a visionary who believed that new energy discoveries would bring plentiful energy to every corner of the earth, creating a better world for all people.

I returned to Capitol Hill and worked for several members of Congress including two women, Congresswoman Marjorie Margoles Mezvenski and Congresswoman Corrine Brown. My assignments as legislative assistant included securing funding for local projects and for veteran's hospitals and health care clinics, examining comprehensive health care proposals, evaluating foreign affairs events including imprisonment of Americans in Ecuador on drug trafficking or money laundering charges, and energy related issues with Russia and the former Soviet Union. During the 1990s, I traveled to Uganda, Ecuador, Ukraine, Russia, and Turkmenistan. From Capitol Hill, I returned to Florida to work as a consultant with an international corporation and to help elect candidates to local and national political positions using my skill as a speech writer and political writer.

On September 11, 2001, I was working and living on Capitol Hill where I managed a Capitol Hill intern program, when the terrorist attacks exploded into New York skyscrapers and the Pentagon. I was disturbed, not only that they happened, but that they happened with such ease. The year before, I worked the Gore 2000 campaign in north Florida and was still reeling from an election in which Florida made international news with its election scandals. I had tried with numerous other concerned citizens to get thousands of votes from an urban Democrat area of Jacksonville to be counted as official votes. In this one particular area of Jacksonville, largely blue collar and strongly Democrat, the thousands of votes had been discarded by the Supervisor of Elections who found no remedy for the discarded votes. Without explanation, they were never shown to the public and never counted.

In the Southeast, George Bush had aligned himself with Christian Evangelicals who considered him to be God's personal appointee to the White House. He touted himself as a devout Christian. The great Christian evangelist Billy Graham, at his Jacksonville crusade just before the presidential election, made known his personal friendship with the Bush family to the thousands of people in the audience. I was becoming unhappy with the Southern Christian notion of "salvation" wedded together with Texas oil money and power. Bush was all about oil money and war. There was never a doubt in my mind. He was willing to sacrifice thousands of lives to gain an oil stake in Iraq. He would do anything to get there. No one seemed to remember that America had been building Saudi Arabia for more than fifty years; Saudi was now blowing itself apart.

I went back to my notes from my time in the middle east in the 1970s and began to read them. Then I began to write them into the stories that had lived with me for so long. It was as if I was back again in Beirut or Egypt or Riyadh or Jeddah or Jerusalem or Tel Aviv. In my mind the importance of the election subsided as I considered the whole of world politics with thousands of years of history. And I knew what I have known for so long; the future is in the hands of women. For thousands of years, men have stood at the forefront of world events with women in the background. Without a doubt, that is changing. Probably Eve, and even Adam, always knew that it was to be so. In Genesis, Eve is portrayed as the final act of God's creation who carried the world's redemption within her own body. Perhaps Eve's time has finally come as we wed technology with the mind of women. In the end, it should be the work of men and women together, across barriers of race and religion, that saves us all!

The middle east became a place for me where daily events were compiled as stories in my head, perhaps to be told one day. Some I wrote down; others now remain locked away, although my writing about those years brings to mind memories long forgotten. The stories of desert days and nights compiled here are meant to give the reader some sense of what the tunnel was like and how I survived it all. I entered the "old world" at the Rome airport in 1973. It was like entering a long, winding tunnel. I departed the "old world" from the airport in Tel Aviv, Israel in 1982, but continued my middle east studies into 1983.

Studying "early art history" in Italy, before coming to Riyadh, expanded my mind to include writings, paintings, sculptures, architecture, culture, and religion throughout places of the "old world" such as Italy, France, Greece, Egypt, Lebanon, Jordan, and Iraq. I was intrigued by maps, caravan routes, and the old cities of Babylon, Cairo, and Jerusalem. The Bible stories that interested me when I was a child suddenly had their own history and texture when placed transparent over layers of early civilization throughout this ancient region. When I finally walked out of the painting in 1982, I entered a whole new life. There was no road back to the former me that existed before 1973; young and, oh so innocent, she passed away so that I might survive the journey. I graduated from University of Maryland in 1984, the same year I began work on Capitol Hill in Washington, DC.

It was not until August 2003, some thirty years after first landing at Rome airport, that I began writing this book. It began as simply digging into a box to bring out pages that are yellow-brown from age. However, the manual typewriter I wrote with so long ago did a good job of putting ink upon page. The words, like me, survived the journey. With pages in hand, I began writing what I intended to be part of a family history for my children, Allen and Preston, and my grandson Starnes. But with September 11, 2001, as part of recent history, I found myself looking through a prism that now includes Saudi attackers slamming into New York skyscrapers, the Washington Pentagon, and the hard Pennsylvania earth. America's response was to attack Iraq; once more placating the Saudi oil barons.

Even as I write today, Saudi Arabia is in the international news. The Wadi Hanifa compound, where I once lived in the late 1970s and managed Army Corps of Engineer events in the compound's recreation center, has, I believe, been ripped apart by explosions. It is difficult for me to know for certain if it is the very compound, but it certainly is possible because of the news photos on the Internet and because of the location. The swimming pool where we gathered with family and friends is located here also. Preston became a ping pong champion here! It is strange to be writing from my notes, while viewing on the Internet a compound ripped apart by terrorists' explosions. When will it ever end? Meanwhile, America is on its own difficult journey, exiting Saudi Arabia while placing armed forces in Iraq and Afghanistan and who knows where else in the Middle East. The global card game continues; as one hand folds another is dealt. If we play long enough and hard enough and drop enough bombs and kill enough people (our own and others) and pay out enough money, maybe we will win.

Somewhere there must be eyes trained to see through the prism. Surprise! Looking back, Saudi Arabia never was a culture sympathetic to western culture and democratic societies. It is fundamentalist, course, dry, dogmatic, and cuts through to the present evil at hand without trials or juries. Its harsh way of life was born in the desert and is uncompromising with foreign ways. Its strongest fundamentalists do not fear direct frontal attack against "the enemy" or insidious religious insult aimed at people and nations who have different beliefs. Nevertheless, in spite of their ancient way of life, progress is upon them. Time has run out for them. I once asked a Saudi man if Saudi women would ever be allowed to drive. He answered that one day they would be allowed to drive. I asked him when that time would come. He seemed amused that I did not have the answer. Finally he answered my question, "They will drive when they decide they want to drive."

Perhaps the answers are all that simple. Change will come at the designated time, with or without US insistence. Meanwhile, we Americans cannot stop the progress of our own nation. We must not continue to play out the same old Middle East games. If we do not change our own tactics, one day we will wake up and realize that the rest of the world (including the Saudis) changed, grew up, modernized, and passed us by.

Focus on America
The other side of my desert journey is less about Saudi Arabia and more about America. America's direction is what interests me today. If it becomes a country that strangles freedom in the name of fear, that uses fundamentalist religion to restrict basic civil rights by promoting a militant restrictive political agenda, that desires to be a theocratic republic (following the example of Islamic republics) rather than a democracy, then America will trade away its own birthright.

I leave the reader with a question. How will America play out its own religious/political agenda? I conclude with the historic Jesus. The moment of truth for me regarding Jesus is more about who he was not. Jesus was not a political warrior; he was a spiritual giant. He was not a religious zealot; he was killed by religious zealots who feared his teaching about life, love, and peace. He said to the world, loud and clear, that God loves peacemakers. Finally, Jesus liked and respected women. He first revealed that he was the savior sought by the Jews to a woman; he drew a line in the sand at a nasty stoning event, saved a woman from men who would kill her, and watched them walk away. One of the women that he was close to was a best friend; she stayed with Jesus until the end of the journey -- which began a new story.

The Energy Question -- A Legislative Strategy

I find that I cannot end this book without addressing the question of energy. First of all, without strong U.S. leadership and a national resolve to create and implement an innovative energy policy, nothing is going to change our "energy business as usual" mentality. Now is the time to think out of the box about the future of our nation's energy resources.

Having assisted the drafting of successful legislation on Capitol Hill, I envision an energy bill, like no previous bill, designed to bring about major U.S. changes. One can hope that a rethinking of our priorities will produce an innovative energy industry capable of improving American lifestyle at home and in the workplace while putting America first in the world in energy technology. Considering the need for such constructive legislation, it is regrettable that DOE has chosen, instead, to maintain the status quo while the U.S. drifts deeper into an international energy crisis. Instead of lack of vision, the U.S. needs global vision in energy technology. How well we master energy technologies will affect how well we run our modern economy and the competitiveness of America's labor force. Undoubtedly, new technologies will lead to the development of a U.S. industry with global commercial benefits.

Legislative Directive -- This bill will be known as the <u>Department of Energy's "Ten Year Plan To End U.S. Dependence on Oil-Based Energy"</u> *"Department of Energy (DOE), responsible for energy programs ranging from nuclear weapons production to Strategic Petroleum Reserves to energy efficiency, should implement a ten year plan to end America's dependence on foreign oil and on oil-based energy. The heart of the strategy would be to create a modern, efficient, comprehensive, and globally-conscious US energy industry to launch America well into the 21st century."*

Part One -- An Energy Campaign with An Education Focus

DOE will direct a comprehensive energy campaign known as the US Energy Campaign (USEC). A USEC panel of advisors, headed by the Secretary of Energy, would comprise advisors from the Department of Defense, the National Science Foundation, Sierra Club, Department of Education, together with leading university academicians, private sector innovators, and Members of the US Congress who chair and are ranking members of pertinent Congressional Committees. Included in the USEC Panel of Advisors would be selected state governors and city mayors representing various regions of the country.

The purpose of the USEC panel would be to direct, manage, coordinate, and implement a comprehensive energy program with ties to other government agencies. The legislation should begin by stating that Americans will be provided the education and training that is necessary to bring about this national energy program. Part One of the bill will provide for (1) greater emphasis on math and science training in elementary and secondary schools for all students, (2) government-funded engineering and science programs at college level focused on innovative energy studies, (3) strengthening links between academic and industrial research at state and regional levels, and (4) retraining America's work force. The provisions would insure that there will be a pool of scientists, engineers, artists and writers, along with an educated work force, to develop modern theories and devise innovative methods for converting ideas into processes that will be commercially viable. Any further Department of Defense (DOD) base closings would transfer these facilities to DOE as education, training, and research facilities.

Part Two -- Funding Priorities

Part Two of the USEC legislation will state that funding priorities will be given to technologies that improve quality of life by improving air, land, and water quality. If, for instance, solar energy is considered such an appropriate energy to pursue, then the processes for devising solar energy cells or other necessary solar products must be through the use of clean technologies. Any legislative proposal will state clearly that air, land, and water quality will not be compromised but will benefit from the technology.

Part Three -- Funding and Personnel Resources

Part Three will provide for extensive program funding and additional personnel requirements. The funding will come about by (1) redirecting research and development funding, along with scientists and engineers, from the DOD to DOE (2) restoring energy-related tax incentives for homes, offices, transportation industries (3) perhaps, placing a tax on gasoline to bring US gasoline prices more in line with those of Europe and Japan. Part Three also will empower DOE to oversee and direct recruitment from DOD while coordinating with the Joint Chiefs of Staff. Additionally, defense contractors would be encouraged to use alternative energy sources for commercial and government use. Additional office space or facilities required for this program will be obtained by converting DOD facilities.

Part Four -- DOE Management Authority

Part Four of the legislation will address specific programs that should be funded and managed by DOE including the establishment of *National Innovative Energy Laboratories* (NIEL) at regional research centers such as Stanford University's Center for Integrated Systems. At regional NIEL centers, research and development activities will lead to energy industry diversification that is both vertical (developing products that are both inputs and outputs) and horizontal (collaboration among industry groups). The research will lead to the development of a new energy industry equipped with the necessary scientific foundation, tools, materials, factories, labor, skills, market research, and global expertise. Transportation projects will be a serious part of DOE's program. Working closely with the Department of Transportation, DOE laboratories will assist in creating efficient technologies enabling high speed rail to connect major cities from coast to coast. These rail systems, in turn, will connect with "over the road" transport systems and international air transport systems. Such integrated transportation systems will be fueled by clean technologies and modern oil-free engines (perhaps fueled by filtered ocean water or by wind or packets of light) that do not yet exist. I envision artists creating such novel ideas on drawing boards, writers explaining how they must work, and innovative science making it all happen. The massive amount of energy-related design, research, and construction projects taking place over the next ten years will be like nothing this country has seen. Meanwhile, America's children will absorb the country's dedication to good ideas, hard work, prudent spending, and investment in their own future. Their own research projects can begin at the earliest grade levels. At the same time, one would hope that the entertainment industry will produce fewer movies about violence and war and more movies about creative and innovative ideas. However, none of this will ever happen if America does not have the leadership and the national resolve to take the first steps.

UNVEILINGS
A Desert Journey
by
Patricia Adora Clark Taylor

POLITICAL OVERVIEW

During World War II, British troops used Egypt as a base for Allied operations throughout the region. British troops were withdrawn to the Suez Canal area in 1947, but anti-British feelings continued to grow after the war. **Lt. Col. Gamal Abdel Nasser overthrew Egypt's King Farouk**, whom the military blamed for Egypt's poor performance in the 1948 war with Israel. **Egypt was declared a republic in 1953.** The same year a **US military training mission was established in The Kingdom of Saudi Arabia at Dhahran**, providing training and support in the use of weapons and other security-related services to the Saudi Armed forces. The **US Army Corps of Engineers** has had a long-term role in military and civilian construction activities in the Kingdom. Saudi Arabia is a Sunni Muslim nation.

DECADE OF THE 1960s -- Chet and I leave Cape Canaveral, Florida for Okinawa
In the 1960s, the US became involved in an ill-fated war with Viet Nam. (The Viet Nam Memorial in our nation's capital is a grim reminder.) Before we could exit that war, the Middle East was heating up fast and drawing the U.S. into a place of huge military build-up and never ending conflict. 1967, long before Chet and I even thought about living in the Middle East, we lived on Okinawa, now part of the Japanese Islands. Preston was born in 1968 at Kadena Air Base Hospital on Okinawa. About the time we landed on Okinawa where Chet would build U.S. air base runways and facilities, Egyptian President Nassar's foreign and military policies helped provoke the Israeli attack of June 1967 that destroyed Egypt's armed forces. During that war, the Middle East went through an incredible change! Israel gained control of the West Bank and all of Jerusalem. The conflict became known as the **Six-Day War**.

Palestinians fled to Jordan from the West Bank to escape the war. Jordan's Palestinian refugee population grew by 300,000; the Palestine Liberation Organization (PLO) was empowered during this time. A major guerrilla-government confrontation occurred in November 1968 when Jordan's government tried to disarm Palestinian refugee camps. Clashes continued throughout the summer of 1970 with the guerrilla groups controlling strategic positions in Jordan. A civil war followed; September was a bloody month when Arabs on both sides were killed. The confrontation was later known as "Black September." In October King Hussein and Yasser Arafat signed an agreement to recognize Jordanian sovereignty and to withdraw armed forces from towns and villages. Israel was blamed for the plight of Palestinian refugees without a homeland; the Middle East became a place of discontent and rage.

DECADE OF THE 1970s -- Chet and I Move to Italy and Saudi Arabia
In the early 1970s, Jordan's neighbor Lebanon had difficulty with the growing presence of Palestinian refugees; at the same time in Lebanon, Muslim and Christian differences grew more intense. Meanwhile, events were heating up in Egypt. After Nassar's death in 1970, Vice President Anwar Sadat became President of Egypt. Sadat conducted a treaty of friendship with the Soviet Union; a year later, he kicked the Soviets out of Egypt. In

1973, the year Chet and I and the boys first landed in Italy, the **1973 Arab-Israeli War** was launched by armies of Syria and Egypt in an attack against Israel. Israel pushed invading armies back beyond the 1967 cease-fire line. The United States and the Soviet Union helped bring an end to the fighting. During the 1973 Arab-Israeli War, Saudi Arabia participated in the **Arab oil boycott** of the United States. After the 1973 war, the rising price of Saudi oil increased Saudi Arabia's wealth and international influence. During this time in Italy, Chet and I could not get heating oil for our house. In 1974, I was touring in Lebanon with the Camp Darby tour group when we saw military tanks in the street in Beruit. Civil war broke out in Lebanon in April 1975. Meanwhile, Saudi Arabia's King Faisal was assassinated by a nephew. Faisal was succeeded by his half-brother Khalid; their half-brother Prince Fahd was named Crown Prince. In Lebanon, Palestinian forces joined Muslim forces in persistent fighting. Lebanon's president called for support from Syrian troops in June 1976. In the fall of 1976, after Arab summits in Riyadh and Cairo, an uneasy quiet settled over Beirut. By this time, our family had relocated to Riyadh.

1976 RIYADH NEIGHBORHOOD NEAR OUR FOUR-FAMILY COMPOUND

In November 1977, Egyptian President Anwar Sadat made a historic visit to Jerusalem, seeking peace through negotiations; the door opened for the 1978 Israeli-Egyptian peace summit convened at Camp David by President Carter. During this time, Chet and I were living in Riyadh; our many friends included Nahed and Salah. There was much excitement about President Sadat's visit to Jerusalem. In May of 1978, I visited Cairo and Alexandria with Nahed. During 1978 President Jimmy Carter invited President Sadat and Prime Minister Begin to join him in trilateral negotiations at Camp David. The Camp David accords were signed September 17, 1978. Sadat's efforts to make peace with Israel earned him the respect of most other Arab states and of much of the world. Saudi Arabia rejected the Camp David accords, claiming that they would not ensure Palestinian rights. (Although Saudi Arabia broke diplomatic relations with and suspended aid to Egypt because of Camp David, the two countries renewed formal ties in

1987.)

In Iran, turmoil ruled as a result of religious and political opposition to the Shah of Iran's rule. The same year, Israel invaded Lebanon in March after a PLO attack on a bus in northern Israel. Later in the year, Israel withdrew, turning over positions to an ally, the South Lebanon Army, and creating a 12 mile wide "security zone."

1979 -- Negotiations led to a 1979 peace treaty between Israel and Egypt signed by President Sadat of Egypt and Prime Minister Menahem Begin of Israel. As a result, Israel withdrew from the Sinai in May 1982.

In January 1979, the Shah of Iran fled for his life, followed by American and western civilians employed in Iran. February 1, 1979, exiled religious leader Ayatollah Ruhollah Khomeini returned from France to direct a revolution and install a theocratic republic guided by Islamic principles. After 15 years in exile Khomeini returned to become Iran's domineering religious leader! About this time Preston and I were delayed at the airport in Dhahran trying to get to the States for a family funeral. Flights were delayed because many were being redirected to Iran to rescue Americans. When Preston and I finally got to Germany en route to the States, we were surrounded by escaping Americans arriving from Iran.

DECADE OF THE 1980s -- CHET AND I MOVE TO ISRAEL TO FINALIZE OUR MIDDLE EAST JOURNEY

On October 6, 1981, just as our family arrives in Israel for a peace keeping mission, President Sadat was assassinated by Islamic extremists in Cairo. Vice President Hosni Mubarak was elected President and maintained Egypt's commitment to the Camp David peace process. Iran continued to spread its Islamic revolution and supported a plot to overthrow the Bahrain Government. In Lebanon, an interim cease-fire brokered by the U.S. between Syria, the PLO, and Israel lasted for a year.

In May 1982, Israel returned the Sinai to Egypt! It was a great time in Middle East history. One month later, in June 1982, we departed Israel, having completed the peace keeping mission, just as Israel invaded Lebanon to fight the forces of Yasser Arafat's Palestine Liberation Organization. Israel moved into Lebanon as far as East Beruit with the help of Maronite Christian leaders and militia. This is when I visited Ron at the hospital near the Lebanese border. During this invasion, Lebanese Christian militias massacred almost 800 Palestinian civilians in the Sabra and Shatila refugee camps. In 1982, the terrorist group, Hizballah emerged in Lebanon from a loose coalition of Shi'a Islamic groups. Hizballah was supported by Syria and Iran.

On May 17, 1983, Lebanon, Israel, and the U.S. signed an agreement on Israeli withdrawal that was conditioned on the departure of Syrian troops. Lebanon's sixteen year civil war left 800,000 people either dead, handicapped, or displaced from their homes. Syria opposed the agreement. Within months, the agreement was canceled; and U.S. Marines, stationed in Lebanon to help keep the peace, departed Lebanon. This same year, terrorist attacks included the April 18, 1983 suicide attack at the US Embassy in

West Beruit and the bombing of American University of Beruit. In 1987, Iranian pilgrims rioted during the Hajj (Islamic pilgrimage) in Mecca, Saudi Arabia.

1990s -- In 1990-91, King Fahd of Saudi Arabia played a key role before and during the Gulf War by helping consolidate forces against Iraq. During and after the Gulf War, the Government of Saudi Arabia provided water, food, shelter, and fuel for coalition forces in the region. There also were monetary payments to the United States and some coalition partners. Egypt also helped assemble the international coalition and deployed Egyptian troops against Iraq. During the 1990s, Lebanese troops moved against Sunni Muslim extremists in northern Lebanon; the extremists now are linked to the Al-Qaeda network. During the Clinton administration, Jordan negotiated an end to hostilities with Israel in 1994 and signed a peace treaty in 1994. Its 1994 treaty with Israel allowed for a continuing Jordanian role in Muslim holy places in Jerusalem.

2000 -- In November, Vice President Al Gore wins the popular vote in a close U.S. 2000 presidential election. In December, a Supreme Court ruling enables Republican George Bush to become the winner. The new president has an abrasive attitude towards foreign policy. Within a few months, on September 11, 2001, Al-Qaeda terrorists (mostly Saudis) proceed with four air strikes against New York and Washington, D.C. without official US interference. Three of the strikes are successful. One plane crashed in Pennsylvania; apparently brought down by passengers who attacked terrorists on the plane. We learn that Al-Qaeda's goal is to defeat U.S. control throughout the Middle East region.

2002 -- President Bush, without United Nations confirmation or approval, orders the United States military to invade Iraq, claiming the country has weapons of mass destruction and is a haven for terrorist organizations. The Republican controlled U.S. Congress gives the Bush Administration what is demanded with little objection from Democrats. In 2003, non-negotiated contracts for rebuilding Iraq go to Bush Administration top officials and friends. U.S. taxpayers are required to fund the U.S. war with Iraq and the rebuilding of Iraq.

At the same time, the U.S., after fifty years in Saudi Arabia, begins shutting down official offices in Riyadh. In November 2003, in Riyadh, Islamic extremists using car bombs blow up part of a two hundred unit compound, known as B-2 in Wadi Hanifa, killing many residents. Formerly, I believe the compound was home to Americans working in Saudi; later it became a compound for diplomats and their families. The compound allows men and women and families to interact with one another; the idea is unacceptable to Islamic fundamentalists. The B-2 explosion is part of a series of explosions taking place throughout Riyadh aimed at frightening people into compliance with restrictive beliefs of Islamic fundamentalists. Al-Qaeda terror network claims responsibility for the B-2 suicide car bombing in Wadi Hanifa.

December 12, 2003, Saddam Hussein is captured by American soldiers in Iraq. The capture is welcome news to many people around the world. The anticipated trial is set for some future date. The success of the capture is marred only by the fact that the outcome of events often turns out differently than one expects in Middle East policy, planning, and strategy.

UNVEILINGS
A Desert Journey
by
Patricia Adora Clark Taylor

US-SAUDI ALLIANCE
And
SEPTEMBER 11, 2001

The Way I See It
The building of America in the twentieth century was all about the US-Saudi alliance. Throughout most of the century, the stakes were high for nations acquiring quality petroleum at the best price! During that time, the US-Saudi alliance was crafted over decades involving expansive US government and US business plans, preparations, and negations intended to build two empires with powerful results in the Middle East region and in the western world. In the west, America, as Saudi Arabia's strong partner, would have high quality petroleum at the best price and would become a political and economic giant; in the east, Saudi would become a regional power and a Moslem showcase to the world. America played the game well, staying in the good graces of the Saudi royal family.

Washington, DC; September 11, 2001
The day of September 11, 2001, and the days following unfolded like a well-written book. Very soon the world knew that Saudi Arabian terrorists made the attack on America. The day of the attack, I was living and working on Capitol Hill in Washington, DC. That morning I heard people shouting and screaming as they ran through the streets; later that day I watched in awe as US military tanks rolled down Massachusetts Avenue. This ridiculous archaic display of our military might was reminiscent of crude World War II military displays in countries ruled by dictators. Where was the US Air Force that day to fight effectively against terrorists in the air? Where was the intelligence community? How was it that two of the tallest buildings in New York, along with the Pentagon in Washington, DC, just happened to be hit that day? New York's mayor was on duty that day, but where was America's president?

The air strikes came exactly as planned, without interference or resistance from any American officials. Ordinary citizens became heroes that day. Only one airplane of the four attack planes missed its final destination, not because of our military might, but apparently because passengers on the plane refused to yield to the madness of mass killers. They took the plane down. The attack on America happened within an hour; then it was over and done. In my opinion, it was not necessary for the Saudis or other terrorists to ever strike again because the plan was completed that day. Afterwards, the missing US president made sure the man who engineered the plan would have safe passage for his family out of the United States. The bin Laden family was safe on a day that thousands of Americans died.

The US-Saudi alliance provided the funds to train the terrorists, ensuring victory.

America's president accused Iraq of the crime and sent troops into Iraq with a splendid display of rockets, much like fireworks, reflected on television around the world. Meanwhile America's president was awarding billion dollar contracts, paid by America's taxpayers, to his daddy's corporation and the corporations of his administration chiefs and his good friends. Unfortunately, newscasters and other media could not bring themselves to even mention Saudi Arabia. Iraq was the culprit! Iraq had weapons of mass destruction! Opps! Maybe that was North Korea. Next, Iran was to be feared; it was on the move against the United States. But where were the Saudis? They were playing dead -- out of sight, out of mind. Saudi Arabia no longer had to worry about brash Iraqi neighbors.

Meanwhile, Saudi Arabia was touted as a splendid nation. Thanks to the US-Saudi alliance, Saudi Arabia had modern cities and military bases; they were armed with American military tactics and the latest weapons. In a quiet, modest way, Saudi could funnel money into terrorist organizations that would strike at the world. For decades, Saudi Arabia received a cash fortune from America; the Saudis gave up nothing. They did not build a democratic society; they did not free their women; they did not ever respect America or want to be American in any way.

Playing the Saudi Game
The roots of September 11, 2001, go back, at least, to the first Arab oil embargo in 1973 when American policy, immature and arrogant, refused to read the changes in global political power. Events that year signaled to the world that there was a growing oil power structure in the Middle East that would defy the west. America turned a blind eye and refused to build its own energy industry, providing no sensible counter to growing oil power. America only wished to go deeper into an alliance with Saudi Arabia, giving Americans a false sense of security. One of the outcomes was that America almost lost its automobile industry on the drawing board because designers refused to design fuel efficient cars. Japanese auto designers were ready to take the US auto market. Toyota, a leader in fuel efficiency, took the industry by storm! Meanwhile, in Washington, there was no creative, positive leadership. In the 1980s, Americans fought a costly Middle East war that was never won. Bitter partisan political battles in the 1990s highlighted America's refusal to grow up and face real global dangers. While we touted the importance of morality, our caustic religious and political leaders refused to see the beam in our own eyes. Much of the world was oil starved; we reveled in oil gluttony at any price. Finally, America was forced to learn that there is no "cheap oil."

Thirty years have passed since I lived in Italy in 1973 and could not get heating oil in the dead of winter when snow covered the ground. Italy, like much of the world, took very real measures toward conservation. Cars with even-numbered or odd-numbered license plates swapped off on which days they could or could not drive on the roads. On Sundays, cars on the road were only for emergencies. It was wonderful! Many streets were open to pedestrians who took full advantage of the opportunity. Our family joined Italian families in Tirrenia strolling down the middle of one of the streets closed to all traffic; many families pushed baby carriages stuffed with warm colorful blankets wrapped around beautiful babies. Everyone was dressed in their Sunday best, generally consisting of warm cotton and woolen clothing. That same year America's fashion statement was polyester suits worn by overweight Americans.

Eleven years later, in 1984, I began working on Capitol Hill. Ronald Reagan, having defeated President Jimmy Carter, was in the White House with little regard for alternative energy; he continued making deals with the Saudis for inexpensive oil. It was the normal American response. After Jimmy Carter's presidency, there was no president who seemed to understand the need to find replacements, not just for foreign oil, but for petroleum as energy. During my Capitol Hill years, first in the 1980s and later in the 1990s, Saudi Arabia remained a mystery to most people working on the Hill. Even after air strikes of September 11, 2001, I believe there is little change.

As for Saudi Arabia, the central institution of Saudi Arabian government continues to be the monarchy. There are no real political parties or national elections. The Qur'an is the constitution of the country, which is governed on the basis of Islamic law (Shari'a). There is continued discrimination against women and ethnic and religious minorities. Throughout the Middle East region, in spite of U.S. intervention and negotiations, the situation has deteriorated in the region. Today, with the situation in Iraq, the U.S. is drawn more and more into a never ending conflict. The great hope of the American people seems to be that, in Iraq, the US will have a stabilizing effect upon the country and the region. Time will tell. However, the fact that the U.S. went into Iraq touting false accusations does not speak well for our own moral leadership. This very same leadership derives direct financial benefit from the war at the expense of dying Americans and the American taxpayer. America is traveling a very dangerous road. The rest of the world most likely will have no problem with the U.S. being sucked into the region; we did it to ourselves. America lied its way into Iraq; there is no way of knowing what price we will pay to get out. Meanwhile, Iraq has a long and brilliant history; it is not going away. Eventually, others will come in after us and run the show.

As for my own family, Preston is thirty-five and lives in Dallas; Preston's son Starnes is twelve years of age, older than Preston when we lived in Saudi. Allen, now known as Al, is forty and lives in Tennessee near Chet's burial site in the beautiful Tennessee hills. Preston, Al, and I have gone on with our lives, but the memories of our many middle east experiences live on in our hearts and minds. When we get together, our conversations are lively with memories about adventurous, intelligent individuals who lived and worked in Saudi Arabia and Israel. Finally, we continue to pray for peace for the United States, for Jerusalem, for Cairo, for Riyadh, for the region, and for the world.

UNVEILINGS
A Desert Journey
by
Patricia Adora Clark Taylor

ABOUT THE AUTHOR...
At age sixteen, Patricia was elected "Governor of Florida Girls' State" and was appointed Co-Chairman of Florida Governor Leroy Collins' Youth Advisory Council. While still in high school, Patricia represented the youth of Florida at the 1958 White House Conference Planning on Children and Youth where she joined youth representatives from across the nation; she was the only female representative. A true pioneer in gender relations, she also assisted Governor Collins with youth related issues at a time when integration of the public schools in Florida was top priority. Soon afterwards, Patricia traveled the world, working with international companies such as Revlon. She graduated from University of Maryland and received a graduate degree from Duke University. She was married to Chester Taylor, a professional engineer (now deceased) with a long, successful, and distinguished career with the U.S. Army Corps of Engineers. Their children, Preston and Al, grew up living in the Pacific Rim, in Europe, and in the Middle East. Patricia's book, Unveilings: A Desert Journey: 1973 – 1983, details their years in Europe and the Middle East. In 1982, while living in Tel Aviv, Israel, Patricia and her husband each received Certificates of Achievement for "contributing to peace in the Middle East."

Patricia's extensive knowledge of culture, science, religion, art, and politics, allows her to blend conflicting, and difficult parts of a project into a worthwhile and memorable success. Her skill and ability can be seen in the establishment of Florida's Timucuan National Preserve which she initiated in 1984 with U. S. Congressman Charles Bennett of Jacksonville, Florida who authored eight books on Timucuan Indian culture and early Florida history. While working as legislative assistant in his Washington office, Patricia drafted legislative language for the Legislative Counsel who wrote the bill. Patricia, providing necessary witnesses and testimony for the House of Representatives Interior Committee, worked closely with the National Park Service, with university professors and other experts knowledgeable about the delicate balance of Northeast Florida and Southeast Georgia ecosystems, and with Florida politicians. Such efforts initiated a legislative success and created a now well-known preserve in Jacksonville visited by tourists from around the world.

In the late 1980s, Patricia departed Capitol Hill, met Ross Perot, and began working with Electronic Data Systems (EDS) in the banking industry group as market analyst and account manager. She secured EDS meetings with the Federal Reserve System and managed the EDS response to the Federal Reserve's "Request for Information" to pre-qualify EDS for systems integration work with the Federal Reserve. In 1990, Patricia relocated to North Carolina for graduate study at Duke University where she received a Master of Liberal Arts Degree for her international study of the history of science. She returned to Capitol Hill. During the decade of the 90s, Patricia's legislative work covered the major issues of our time from health care reform to international events, taking her on investigative trips to the former Soviet Union, Africa, and Ecuador. Recently, Patricia was part of an international team to monitor a presidential election in West Africa

After years of traveling the world and living on Capitol Hill, Patricia recently bought a home in Jacksonville and relocated to her home town. Today she is a grandmother, writer, artist, and consultant. Her favorite pastimes are taking long walks on the beach, becoming reacquainted with old friends, and meeting new friends.

About Unveilings, Patricia says, "I had the courage to write it from my notes written during the 1970s and early 80s. I was so young! Only recently have I begun to see patterns in my life and in international events that cause me to see a much larger picture."